I0076629

Scaling Up Your Job Search

Three Strategic Steps to Landing Your Ideal Job

Tom Nosal

Copyright © 2014 by Tom Nosal

All rights reserved. No part of this publication may be reproduced, distributed, or transmitted in any form or by any means, including photocopying, recording, or other electronic or mechanical methods, without the prior written permission of the publisher, except in the case of brief quotations embodied in critical reviews and certain other noncommercial uses permitted by copyright law.

This book is designed to provide information and motivation to our readers. It is sold with the understanding that the publisher is not engaged to render any type of psychological, legal, or any other kind of professional advice. The content of each article is the sole expression and opinion of its author, and not necessarily that of the publisher. No warranties or guarantees are expressed or implied by the publisher's or author's choice to include any of the content in this book. The advice and strategies contained herein may not be suitable for your situation. You should consult with a professional where appropriate.
Neither the publisher nor the individual author shall be liable for any physical, psychological, emotional, financial, or commercial damages, including, but not limited to, special, incidental, consequential or other damages. Our views and rights are the same: You are responsible for your own choices, actions, and results.
If you do not wish to be bound by the above, you may return this book to the publisher for a full refund.

Printed in the United States of America
First Printing, 2014
ISBN 978-0-615-99095-8

Scaling Up, Inc
www.scalingupsuccess.com

Table of Contents

Forward   xiii

Introduction   xvii

Step One – Getting Started

Chapter 1
So You've Lost Your Job....Now What?   1

Chapter 2
Taking Inventory   7

Chapter 3
List of Needs   13

Chapter 4
Setting Goals   17

Chapter 5
Vision   21

Chapter 6
Tell Everyone   25

Chapter 7
Changing Your Mindset   27

Step Two – Finding a job

Chapter 8
Marketing Yourself   33

Chapter 9
Your Marketing Message   37

Chapter 10
Networking   43

Chapter 11
Volunteering   51

Chapter 12
Job Boards and Job Fairs   59

Chapter 13
Social Media, Email and Personal Websites   65

Chapter 14
Resumes   81

Chapter 15
Cover Letters   91

Chapter 16
Understanding Job Postings and Applying   95

Step Three – Getting the job

Chapter 17
Interviewing   105

Chapter 18
Preparing for the Interview   111

Chapter 19
Preparing for Interview Questions   115

Chapter 20
The Hidden Interview Questions   129

Chapter 21
Stories   135

Chapter 22
Practicing for the Interview   139

Chapter 23
Acing the Interview   143

Chapter 24
The Phone Interview   153

Chapter 25
Other Types of Interviews   157

Chapter 26
Asking for the Job and Following Up   163

Chapter 27
Communication Skill   167

Chapter 28
Selling the Sizzle   173

Chapter 29
Conclusion   175

Resources   179

Acknowledgements   181

"Your work is going to fill a large part of your life, and the only way to be truly satisfied is to do what you believe is great work. And the only way to do great work is to love what you do. If you haven't found it yet, keep looking. Don't settle. As with all matters of the heart, you'll know when you find it."

--Steve Jobs

Forward

Why this Book? Why Now?

I have been coaching job seekers for 5 years now and it still amazes me the number of newly unemployed people I see very month. And even sadder still, the number of people who are still out there searching, for months and even years.

But saddest of all are the number of people out there, good people, intelligent people, hardworking people, who have simply given up on job hunting. They've been at it too long, been out of work too long, and are just too tired to continue. That is the sad state of our job market today.

I cringe every month when the jobs report come out and they announce how 150,000 jobs were added this month, 160,000 added last month and everyone gets a little excited. Except what they don't mention is the fact that 70% or more of these jobs added are low paying jobs, jobs that you can't afford to feed, clothe and raise your family on. Certainly not jobs that allow you to keep your house and live above the poverty level.

They also don't like to mention that while we may add 150,000 jobs a month, we are continuing to lose 50,000 or more jobs a month. People are losing jobs that pay $60,000 a year and finding jobs that pay only $20,000.

The government only keeps statistics on those who are unemployed and collecting benefits. They don't keep track of those whose unemployment has run out or those who just gave up looking for work. The real unemployment numbers are staggering.

I've read reports that state how there are millions of jobs available that employers cannot fill. When the number of unemployed people is five to six times greater than the quantity of jobs that are available, you have to wonder how this statistic can be true. Unfortunately it is.

Employers claim that there is a serious shortage of people having the skills they need. Really? All those unemployed people and no one has the skills you are looking for? Well, here's a news flash, maybe the problem is the employer and the way they go about hiring.

Maybe employers should stop letting a software program eliminate half of their candidates and they should take the time to really read the resumes of people who are applying. Maybe that great candidate is out there but you eliminated them because they didn't dot every I and cross every T or they guessed wrong on what keywords your computer is searching for.

Why did I write this book? I wrote it to help job seekers overcome these obstacles. To help you become employed and help employers fill those open positions.

I wrote this book because as I attend other job-seeking events I have an opportunity to listen to what others have to say on the subject. And I began to see a pattern, a pattern of the same old information being reprocessed, rewritten and regurgitated again and again.

As I sat through more and more of these presentations, and learned more about the presenters standing up there and giving advice, I began to notice a serious problem. Most of these people giving advice have never actually hired anyone. So I thought to myself enough is enough. Somebody needs to give these job seekers the information they really need to get a job.

This book will give you a different viewpoint on the job hunting process, and that is from the viewpoint of an actual hiring manager, the person who has the final say in whether or not you get the job. So all the advice contained in this book is designed to get you in front of the final decision maker in the quickest way possible.

This book is not intended to be a primer on the job-hunting process with step-by-step instructions on how to write a cover letter, a resume, or how to apply online to job postings. There is an overabundance of information available to you from other sources and you don't need yet another book telling you how to do those tasks. Although I will tell you how to make those activities work better for you.

If you want to get hired at your ideal company, to work in your ideal position, and to earn a salary that you can live with, then this book is for you; if you are willing to focus your attention, commit yourself to the process and put in the extra effort required.

Like anything in life, your job search will be unique. Your situation is not the same as everyone else's and it is almost impossible to cover every situation in a book. In order to help someone in their unique situation, you need to work one-on-one with a dedicated career coach. A career coach can focus in on you and your unique situation and develop the strategies necessary to help you succeed. If you are committed to getting your career search on the fast track, then go to www.scalingupsuccess.com and fill out your contact information.

Introduction

Whether you are just starting your job search or are a seasoned veteran of the job search process, first of all let me say that I'm sorry about your circumstances. I know how you feel. I've been in your shoes before. But I got over it and past it. And you will too. The only question is: How long is it going to take you?

The answer to that question depends entirely on you. You are the one who can control your future and which path you want to travel down to get employed. You are the one who controls how hard you want to work at finding a new job and what attitude you will have.

It is important to adjust your thinking to realize that you are the one in control of your job search. Not the employer, not the economy, recruiters, friends, family or even your spouse. You control your job search and your results. Realizing that you are in control will change your attitude.

While you control the majority of your job search, there are several things you have no control over. You cannot control if you are invited to interview, if a job offer is extended to you or whether the employer communicates with you. These are all in control of the hiring company. And since you have no control over these situations the best action you can take is to keep moving forward, because you can control how you respond to these situations and how they affect your attitude.

So if your attitude is in the right place and you've gotten past blaming your past employer, the company's you applied to who never got back to you, the government and anyone else you can think of, and if you're ready to accept responsibility and hit this job market head-on, then continue reading.

But let's clarify something first. This book is not for everyone. While I would love everyone to read this book I feel it would be a disservice to you if I did not getting something out into the open.

I need you to really take a moment and read this next paragraph carefully. I mean really carefully because it will set the tone and your expectations for the rest of this book.

If you are the type of person who likes:

- Spending time on the Internet searching job boards
- Spending 20 hours a week or less searching for a job
- Sending out 10 or more resumes a week
- Applying online to countless job openings (real or fake)
- Waiting for weeks for the HR department to call you
- Being mad at the world and has no problem showing the rest of us

Then this book may not be the right resource for you because reading it will probably not do you any good and will more than likely cause you to be uncomfortable. But if you are frustrated with the results you've gotten so far, are unsure of what to do next, your bills are mounting, your patience is wearing thin, and you're not having fun anymore, then by all means continue reading. We'll work together to get you in the right position to get you employed as quickly as possible.

All I ask of you are three things:
1. Read this with an open mind and embrace some new ideas, activities and thought processes
2. Understand that some of the information in this book may make you uncomfortable at first
3. Understand that in the end you still have to be the best person for the job in the mind of the hiring manager

So if you're ready to get going, I'll start by giving you a brief synopsis of my background.

I spent roughly twenty-five years working for various manufacturers of telecommunications equipment. At each company I was employed at, I worked my way up to various management positions. Being a manager, one of my major duties was to recruit, interview, hire, coach and manage employees. I was pretty successful at this. Almost all of the people I hired turned out to be exceptional employees. There were a couple that turned out to be moderate employees, not great but not terrible either.

I was also laid off twice in this industry. The first time was in 1991. I was lucky and found a job within three months. The second time was in 2002. I survived six rounds of lay-offs and I remember thinking "Really, how many more can there be. We've already lost almost half the employees."

But once again I got that much despised call that indicated my services were no longer needed.

Not to worry I thought. I'll get another job soon. I got my last job through networking, I'll get another. Problem being, all of my best contacts in the industry were in my same predicament. They were either all looking for a job or were trying hard to keep theirs.

Having not had to look for a job for many years, I was unprepared for the changes that came about in 2002 on how to get one. One of the first things I did was enroll in college. I had the time now to go on and get a business degree. So I entered college as a freshman at the age of 45. Being the oldest student in my classes was not that hard, but being older than most of the teachers does give you a different perspective.

In my search for answers to solving this mystery of job-hunting, I turned to an executive counseling firm to get me on track, which by the way cost me a lot of money. A lot of money. Basically what I got out of it was a new resume. But I did learn one thing from them, the absolute need to network. While I did learn about the need to network from them, they weren't very good at showing me how to network; something that I will show you in detail in another chapter in this book.

In reality, I really learned how to network when I started doing it for business reasons. I learned by my own trial-and-error and by observing some of the best networkers. I found the absolute best ways to network, where to network, and how to make it work. Since then, I have taught many job seekers and business owners on how to network effectively.

When I was unemployed and searching for the right job, I made a ton of mistakes. And I mean a ton. Mostly because I followed all of the wrong advice. I spent hours on the Internet searching job boards, I applied to every job I could find, I wrote my resume all wrong, and when things got really desperate, I made even more mistakes. Looking back on it, I wish that I had a career coach to help guide me through the correct process and keep me on track. I learned one powerful lesson out of all this, I will never again go without the services of a professional coach and the support of a mastermind group.

Through the ensuing years, I held several part-time and full-time jobs and started a couple of businesses. Both of which turned into non-profits. Not in the IRS sense of a non-profit organization, I just didn't make any money. I am now on my third business and I am loving every minute of it. I absolutely love the coaching business. I love speaking in public, and I am ecstatic when I see my clients achieve success.

Well there you have it. I have hired and coached employees for over twenty years, and have coached job seekers for five years.

While I will touch on some of the basic mechanics you will need to perform your job search, it will not be extremely detailed. I will instead focus on the main philosophy, tactics and processes you absolutely need to conduct a job search today, and that will give you the best chance of getting hired. While I can't guarantee you that following the information in this book will land you a job, I will tell you straight out that using what you learn here will set you miles apart from the other job candidates.

Like anything, there is a plethora of information on how to do just about anything in this world. And the job search process is no different. You can read and go to lectures and take classes on just about anything in the career development industry.

There is information that will contradict someone else. Just like those scientific studies where one study tells you drinking coffee is bad for you, and a different one that tells you drinking coffee is good for you.

So it is with much integrity that I will tell you that you will undoubtedly find information out there that will contradict what I am telling you in this book, and more than likely, several experts as well. I'm okay with that, in fact I enjoy hearing other points of view. Everyone has different backgrounds and personal experiences. The key is to follow the advice that makes sense to you because in the end, you are the person responsible for your career and your future.

I encourage you to choose and commit to a strategy that you believe will achieve your desired results. But no matter which method you choose, this is the best advice I can give you; if it isn't working, change it.

If your previous method is not working, or if you are first starting out in a job search, then I invite you to try my method. It is a compilation of my own management and coaching experience, personal research, and information I've learned from conversations with other business owners and hiring managers.

One last thing. I am not an HR recruiter, nor do I hold advanced degrees in career coaching, Psychology, or Human Resources. I am someone who has a lot of real world experience, who has interviewed and hired some of the highest quality candidates, and who has spent a considerable amount of time learning and observing from the real world. And unlike some of the other experts out there, I've actually recruited, interviewed and hired other people. People just like you.

So let's get started on the path to getting that premium job you've dreamed of.

STEP ONE – Getting Started

"The journey of a thousand miles begins with but a single step."
--Confucius

Chapter One

So You've Lost Your Job...Now What?

"When one door closes, another opens; but we often look so long and so regretfully upon the closed door that we do not see the one which has opened for us."
--Alexander Graham Bell

There are several things you will need to do before you can seriously start your job search.

1. Get over it

Look, you lost your job, most likely through no fault of your own. I get that. I've been there, done that, and have the T-shirt to prove it.

You're not the only one this has happened to. There are several million people in countries all around the world who are in your exact same predicament. Through no fault of their own, they are unemployed and looking for work, watching their savings disappear, unsure what to do next.

Now is the time for you to get over it. If you have not already accepted your current situation, you need to get to that point as quickly as you can and decide to move forward. You cannot conduct a professional successful job search when you are still mad at the world. In order to succeed you need to be objective, friendly, and personable.

The number one attribute that you need to be successful in finding a job is having a positive attitude and I don't mean only during an interview. While that is certainly most important, having a negative attitude will tremendously affect your search. It will keep you from doing the things you need to do, building good relationships and remaining focused.

You will undoubtedly run into many other job seekers during your search who have a crummy disposition, maybe even friends and family members. Ignore them and avoid them whenever you can. Keep a positive attitude and you will get through this.

During your job search I suggest that you form a close support group. This is a group of close friends, family and even fellow job seekers that you can turn to in order to vent your frustrations. It's important to have a group like this in order to keep yourself from burning out. Vent your anger with them and not with other groups. This will allow you to keep a positive attitude in all other aspects of your job search.

And not to rain on your cheery disposition, but the odds are 50/50 that some time in the future, after you get your next job, this may happen again. It's just life. If you want to protect yourself from never being fired from a job again, then maybe you need to think about starting your own business.

2. Decide first and foremost, do I want a job

While this is not the ideal time to think about starting a business, there are several things to consider. One is that you are currently not receiving an income, so the thought of losing any income does not come into play. So this is a perfect opportunity to cut loose and see what happens. But make absolutely sure that is what you want to do.

As I reflect back on my own job search, I realized why I was not having much success. Internally, I really did not want a job. Oh sure, on the outside it appeared that I wanted one, but deep down inside I didn't. I wanted to run my own business and never have another job again. It took me a long time to realize this and if I had really thought this through early in my job-hunting process, I could have saved myself and my family a lot of time and sorrow.

Which is why I strongly suggest that you take the time to make this discovery for yourself. Your life will be a whole lot easier if you know which path you want to travel down. Some people already know they do not want to be in business for themselves and that's great. But if you are unsure of which path to choose, I would highly recommend that you hire a great career coach so that you can travel down this road to discovery together.

And as I look back on the multitude of resumes and cover letters I sent out, I can see it. They were not written as if I wanted the job I applied for. Keep that in your memory banks as you continue through this book.

3. Figure out what you want to be when you grow up

"Adults are always asking little kids what they want to be when they grow up because they're looking for ideas."
--Paula Poundstone

That's right. What do you want to be when you grow up? Decide now before you start going down the wrong path.

Do you want to stay in the same position?
Do you want to stay in the same industry?
Do you want to stay in the same city, county, state?
What would be the best job for you?

You would not believe how many people come to me seeking advice who have no clue what job they are looking for. The usual response is "I don't know. Any job will do." But in reality just any job won't do.

You see it is vitally important that you know <u>EXACTLY</u> what job you are looking for. Otherwise, how will you know when you've found the right one? Today you have to be laser focused on the job you want. It takes a whole lot of time and effort and you want to focus all your energies on getting that job and not just any job. You want the job you want. At this point, I do need to caution you about taking a job that you may not really want.

When you lose your job and have no income the first instinct is to go into survival mode which is only natural. No one would ever fault you for that. But you need to be smart and really think this through before rushing in.

If you take on temporary work, a part-time or seasonal job or work as a contractor to help pay the bills, that is great. It will help ease some of the financial strain. And any employer will understand the reasons you took this job and why you are leaving it. But if you take on a job that is considered more of a permanent job, that's where the problems can come in.

You see there is a huge Catch-22 in the job market and it revolves around the idea that it is easier to find a job if you are already employed. And there is some truth to that statement. If you are still employed and are searching for a new job, it is much easier to explain why you are looking for one.

But if you took on a full-time position at a company and are still continuing to find a better job, it is going to be difficult to explain that situation in a way that will appease another employer, and make you look good. Let's walk through a scenario so that you can understand this concept from a hiring manager's perspective.

Let's say you took on a position at company A that is not your intended profession. You obviously took this position at this company as a stepping stone, a place to land and earn an income while you continue to seek a more suitable employment. If you should land an interview at another company and you explain why you are looking, the first thought that is going to go through the hiring managers mind is: "Is this just another stepping stone for you? Are you going to work here while continuing to look for a better job?" Do you see how this could make you look poorly to another employer?

Additionally, despite what some people think, it is not any easier finding a job if you have a job. You have less time to network, research, write resumes and prepare. Not to mention having to take all that time off for interviewing. Just understand the ramifications of taking on those interim jobs while you continue to look for your ideal position.

And just what does that ideal job look like? Well odds are pretty good, it doesn't look anything like the job description you will find on any website. Or at least that job description certainly does not match up with your skills, and vice-versa.

There are what seems an unending number of personality tests, career tests, success tests, etc. out there that will help you determine what job is best for you. I've taken most of these tests myself, sometimes more than once just to compare results. (River Barge Captain? Really??)

While these are certainly helpful, I'm of the belief that no one and certainly no test, knows what job you want better than you do. The problem is getting that information out of the back of your mind and into the foreground.

So I've devised a little exercise of my own that you can do to make your own career determinations. To find out what really excites you in a job and will help you to focus only on those jobs that offer what you are looking for. Because isn't that what you really want?

Before you start your job search, you need to complete an inventory, take a self-assessment and develop a list of needs.

Chapter Two

Taking Inventory

"Find out what you like doing best and get someone to pay you for doing it."
--Katherine Whitehorn

This step will help you to recognize your skills, develop a resume and prepare for an interview.

The inventory is basically a list of your skills and weaknesses. It is important to know these so that again, you are focusing on the right job and not any job. Taking a self-inventory is a brainstorming activity. The idea is to let the thoughts start flowing out without giving any real thought to them. This is how it works.

Step One:

Make a chart with 5 columns and a whole bunch of rows that looks like this:

Activity	S	W	L	D

If you want to save some time, you can go to my website, **www.scalingupsuccess.com** and download a Word copy.

Use one sheet for each job you ever had starting with your very first job. Yes, this includes the paper route, bagging groceries, washing cars, and babysitting. You will understand why I want you to start there in a little while.

The key to doing this exercise is honesty. You need to be completely honest and open with yourself in filling this out. Look, this is your career we're talking about here, not mine. I already did this. That's how I found my best career. If you're not completely honest with yourself in this activity, the only people you will be hurting is yourself and your family because you are going to wind up with a job that is not right for you. A job that you don't really care about, that you will find a struggle going to every day, one that you will be shortly looking to get out of. I know, I've been there and I don't want to be there again.

So at the top of the page, put the name of the company and the position you held. If you had multiple positions, use a separate sheet for each position. Now under the activity column, list every single activity you did at this job. Think hard. It is important to list as many as you can.

Now once you have listed every activity for that job, you can now start filling out the remaining columns. The column headings should be S (Strength), W(Weakness), L (Like)and D (Dislike). This an explanation for how you should determine where to put a mark:

Strength = This activity is one you are really great at. You do an excellent job at it, make few mistakes and people have told you that you are great at it. It comes up in all your reviews as an excellent rating. You could do this task anywhere with total confidence and feel very comfortable at it.

Weakness = This activity is not one of your better points. You did it as part of your job, or because someone required you to do it. You stumble through it but really don't understand how to do it extremely well. It comes up on annual reviews as "needs improvement". You are not comfortable doing this job anywhere.

Like = Regardless if it is a strength or weakness, you love doing this task. It gets you excited and you have fun doing it. You don't complain about it to anyone or mope about it when you come home. It makes you happy and you feel enriched when doing this task.

Dislike = You hate doing this job. If you were the boss you would pawn this job off on the first person you saw. You gripe about it to coworkers and are still stewing about having to do it when you get home. The dog suffers the consequences because you had to perform this task.

For each activity you listed, make a mark in either the S or W column, and another in either the L or D column. Now you may come across an activity that you list as a strength but that you hate doing, or a weakness that you really like doing. That's okay, mark it as it really is.

You may find some activities that are neither a strength nor a weakness or ones that you neither like nor dislike. That's okay too, just don't check a column for that activity.

When you have finished the page for this employer and job, start a second page for your next position or employer. Keep doing these until you've made a list for every employer and position you've had.

Step Two:

Take all of your activities and start grouping them under functions. Here are some examples of functions you can start grouping:

- Working with customers
- Sales
- Accounting
- Labor
- Filing
- Presenting

The list can go on and on but you will shortly be able to identify the major functions you do in your regular job duties.

What you have completed to this point is a complete inventory of all the job activities and skills you have acquired from your entire work history. This information will become very important later when you are crafting your resume and preparing for job interviews.

While these two steps were important, this next step is by far the most critical for a successful job search.

Step Three – Self Assessment

Take all of the activities you have listed with a checkmark in the L (Like) column and put them together in one spot.

Now find all the ones that you've checked as Like and all the ones you've checked as Strengths and group those together.

Voila! You have just completed a job description for your perfect job. The activities you have listed as both Like and Strength are the jobs you should be pursuing with interest. These are the jobs you are going to be most fulfilled in, will do the best job in, and more importantly will have the easiest time selling to a prospective employer.

You've also identified activities that you like doing but are not necessarily a strength. That's okay. Now is a perfect time to enhance your skills in these areas to make you more marketable. Don't avoid jobs with these activities, just become aware that there are not your strong points and be prepared to answer questions about them during the interview.

Bonus: you've also identified some skills to answer the question; "Tell me about your weaknesses."

Chapter Three

List of Needs

"Decide what you want, decide what you are willing to exchange for it. Establish your priorities and go to work."
--H.L. Hunt

Now that you have identified the kind of work you want to do, you are going to want to put together a list of needs that you want to have in your new job. Some of these needs are going to be absolutes, and some are going to be perks. Your job here is to identify all of these items and rank them in levels of importance.

Because each company and each position are going to have different benefits available to you, it is as important to identify which are great to have and which are going to be deal breakers. The deal breakers are going to be the determining factors on which jobs to apply for at which companies, and the great to haves are bonuses and/or areas of negotiation.

Some of the items you may want to consider in your list of needs are:

- Office Location
- Office Space
- Hours
- Dress Code

- Commute Time
- Parking
- Amount of Travel
- Flex-time
- Work remotely
- Health Care
- Vacation Time
- Holidays
- Child Care

Some of these might be under the control of the company, some are not. But they all will play a role in your decision on whether to apply for or accept a job offer at a company. Make your list as complete as possible.

Once you have completed your list, group them in order of importance. The items that you absolutely need to have should be grouped together as Needs. The rest can be grouped together as perks, or open for negotiation.

Once you have this list of needs completed, there is one more list you need to put together, and that is a list of needs from the company itself. This is another critical list you need to put some deep thought into. Some items to put on this list could include:

- Industry
- Products
- Types of Services
- Headquarters Location
- Company Culture
- Mission and Vision
- Demographics of Employees

- Size of Company
- Management Structure
- Management Style of Immediate Supervisor
- Availability of Manager

You may think this is a silly exercise but this will help you to determine which companies you are going to pursue for your next job because you are not going to settle for just any job at any company. You are going to focus on **THE** job at **THE** company.

And if you don't think this important, let me give you a heads-up here. Any recruiter, hiring manager and interviewer worth their salt is going to spot your enthusiasm in a minute, and determine if you are going to fit in and if you really want this job.

That is why I am taking you through these exercises. There is no need in wasting your time developing a resume, apply for a job and interviewing for a position at a company that you are not totally thrilled about..

It is okay if at the end of the interviewing process you decide this is not the right position for you, but at least go into it with all of the enthusiasm that this is going to be the job for you.

Because if you are not convinced that this is the job for you, there is no way on this earth that you are going to convince a hiring manager of this. And that is why you are not going to get the job.

Chapter Four

Setting Goals

"The trouble with not having a goal is that you can spend your life running up and down the field and never score."
--Bill Copeland

While I have succeeded at a lot of things in my life, I have also failed at a lot of things in my life. When I look back at these events, the number one reason without a doubt for either a success or a failure comes down to this; having a clear focused goal.

When I did not have a clear-cut goal I failed, miserably. When I did have a goal I succeeded.

Now when I talk about a goal, I don't mean a wishy-washy goal, like "Someday, I want to have a job. Any job." I mean a real goal, like "I will have my business open on December 11, 2012."

The same things apply to job hunting. If you don't have a clear-cut laser-focused goal, you will fail at obtaining your ideal job. And that is something you cannot afford to do.

So an example of a laser-focused goal is this: "I will start my new Sales Manager job at ABC, Inc. on December 1, 2014."

So what makes this a laser-focused goal?

1. It starts with an "I will" statement. An "I will" statement removes all hesitation and escape clauses from your mind. There is no try, there is only "I will."
2. It identifies the exact position you will be starting. It does not say any job. It is the specific job you want.
3. It names the company you want to work for. Not any company will do, only ABC company.
4. It gives an exact date. It is not sometime in the future, it is not sometime this year, it is not sometime in December. It is December 1st, 2013.

With this kind of a goal your chances of succeeding are greatly increased. The idea of having this goal cements in your mind a solid plan, one that you can use to play over and over again. One that you can use to make all your decisions from this point forward asking yourself, "Does this activity move me closer to achieving this goal?" If the answer is no, then you should ignore it or put it on hold. If the answer is yes, then move forward.

Two major points about setting your goals for getting a job:

1. They must be achievable. In other words, don't set your goal for getting a job for two weeks, because it is more than likely not possible. But also, do not set it for a year from now.
2. They must be measurable. So if one of your goals is to make three new networking contacts this

week, then you can measure your performance against that goal.

A goal allows you to put a plan together starting with the end goal in mind. If your end goal is to get your new job within six months (which is realistic and achievable), you can develop a plan of what you need to do every day to achieve that goal.

Chapter Five

Vision

"A vision is a clearly-articulated results orientated picture of a future you intend to create. It is a dream with direction."
--Jesse Stoner Zemel

Of course none of this is going to do you much good without having a clear vision of the job you want to achieve. While having a goal helps us understand what it is we want to achieve, a vision keeps us moving in a positive direction and helps us to overcome obstacles that stand in our way, or better yet, helps us to avoid them entirely.

Entrepreneurs, athletes, entertainers, and many other successful people use vision to propel them along and keep them going. A vision is basically a picture that you plant in your head of what it would look like or feel like when you accomplish your goal. For example; when I am going to be speaking to an audience, the first thing I do is envision what that speech is going to look like. I imagine the audience, the room, and I picture myself in front of them giving a successful speech.

What I don't envision is giving a bad speech, being nervous, or forgetting what I am going to say. And because I envision this speech as being successful, I can also take steps to ensure this is going to happen.

You see without the correct vision, your journey is going to be a long and unfruitful one. And you will get sidetracked and start running in circles and getting nowhere.

Think back to a vacation you might have been on in the past. Did you choose your destination because of the airline or the hotel or did you choose it because you pictured yourself in that destination?

And it was probably those visions that you had in your head that kept you heading toward that destination no matter what happened along the way; delayed flights, car problems, screaming children, detours, etc. None of those kept you from getting to that vacation spot. A little late maybe, but you got there.

It is the same thing on your job search. Getting the job you want is the ultimate destination on this journey. All the skills you learn along the way will not mean anything if you don't have the vision of this job firmly cemented in your head.

Once you have focused in on the job you want, you need to develop a picture in your mind of what it will look like. This is what is going to keep you on-track and keep from derailing when you hit a bump in the road.

So implant a vision of yourself in this job:

- What does the office look like?
- What will you be wearing?
- What will you be doing?
- How will the work feel?
- How will you interact with your boss and your coworkers?

- How will your spouse feel when you get this job?
- How will you feel?

Picture yourself: walking into the office, touching the keyboard on your PC, sitting at your desk.

See yourself in the cafeteria. Smell the coffee, feel the newspaper.

Picture how your desk will look and how that chair will feel with you in it. Picture how the carpeting will look and the color of paint on the walls.

Embrace as many images and use as many senses as you can to insert yourself in that picture.

Vision is an extremely powerful tool in reaching your goals. Can you imagine what life would be like if Thomas Edison did not have a vision in his head and quit after the first couple of thousand failed experiments?

The vision you implant in your mind is what's going to get you up in the morning and keep you motivated during the day. That vision will keep you on track toward landing your ideal job and help you push through the disappointments and setbacks that could occur along the way.

Find a quiet place where you can be alone without distractions. Put your feet up and close your eyes. And start to develop that picture in your mind of you and your new job. Then play that movie over and over again. Play it every day.

Some people find it beneficial to put together a vision board. This is basically a collection of pictures that represents what you want in your future. You can paste these pictures onto a poster board and use it to help remind you of your ideal job. Keep it out in the open where you can see it every day.

When I started this business, I started it with a very specific vision, a vision of what I wanted my life to be like in the future. And this vision included having a big boat in some sunny warm location. I have a picture of this boat everywhere. It is in several files, it is the background on my laptop, it's the first thing I see when I open my meeting binder, and it's on my vision board. I can picture this boat in great detail in my mind. More importantly, I have a vision of my wife and me on this boat, relaxing and having fun, and enjoying life.

It is this vision that keeps me moving in a certain direction. There are no shortcuts, side roads or obstacles, just a clear vision to keep me on the right path. I have put together a clear plan on how to achieve this goal.

Use your vision to keep yourself on track during this job hunt and in the future.

Chapter Six

Tell Everyone!

"Tell everyone what you want to do and someone will want to help you do it."
--W. Clement Stone

That's right, announce the fact that you lost your job. Now more than ever you are going to need your closest friends and family members to help you get through this. Losing a job and being unemployed is a very emotional and trying time. It's a social stigma that people find hard to shake. I understand. I felt the same way. Losing a job makes you feel, well bad is one thing. But sometimes it can also be a good thing if you hated your job or were in a very negative environment. There are many different feelings and emotions running around inside you during this time.

Usually the first course of action in this environment is to hide from others. The thought of answering questions with the words "I'm unemployed" or the ever popular "I'm in transition" just sends you clamoring for a closet. So you can hide out and not have to see anyone. I understand. I've been there. I've gone through too many family gatherings having to answer the same old questions time after time. It gets old and wears you down.

Well my antidote for this kind of thinking is to take a different approach. Instead of shying away from going to social gatherings learn to embrace them as an opportunity, an opportunity to meet others and enlist their help.

And the first group that you embrace in this regard is your close circle of family and friends. Your inner circle should be your first line of foot soldiers that you need to get working for you in your job search. Who else besides yourself has a more vested interest in getting you employed?

The usual reaction when you first tell someone that you lost your job is one of sorrow or sadness. Then they will jump into the what can I do to help mode. Let them first digest the information that you lost your job. Then get them primed that you may need their help in the near future. Get them ready to go to battle with you, but don't send them out without ammunition and a clear battle plan.

Warning! It is important that you emphasize that you will let them know what they can do to help. Don't let them go off in directions you are not interested in going in. I've had well-meaning friends and family members set me up with job interviews at places I had no intentions of ever working at. This creates an awkward situation for all parties involved.

When you have finished this book, identified your goals and developed a game plan, then you can start mobilizing your troops in a strategic manner. You can have them make introductions, make inquiries of their friends and co-workers, or any other help you may need from them. Give them the information and direction they need in order to know how to best help you.

Chapter Seven

Changing Your Mindset

"You will never change your actions until you change your mind."
--Van Crouch

Today's job market is a lot different than it was years ago.

First, there are a lot more job seekers then there are jobs available, which makes the competition a lot tougher with more people applying for the same job.

Second, hiring managers are making out a longer shopping list of experience and requirements they are looking for. Not so long ago, a hiring manager would take the time to train someone on their products, industry and even on job functions. That is no longer the case. Today they are looking to hire someone they can just "plug and play." This practice in itself makes no sense. Finding someone with all of the skills and experience to meet the job requirements is difficult, and they will most likely not want to pay this person the salary commensurate with this experience.

Third, there are many hiring managers who are untrained and ill equipped to conduct a smart, sensible job search, and job seekers are ill equipped to compete in this job market.

This book is intended to help job seekers with the latter. (I'll help those hiring managers in another book.)

Not all that long ago, a person looking for a job usually followed a job search that looked something like this:

1. Buy a newspaper
2. Find an interesting job
3. Call or visit the business
4. Interview and hopefully get the job

Today, most job seekers follow this job search method:
1. Write a ridiculously long resume
2. Search on the Internet for a job
3. Email a resume or fill out an online application
4. Wait for someone to call them

More informed job seekers will start networking for a job by attending local job clubs and going to other networking meetings. But even they go about it the wrong way.

To compete productively in today's job market, you need to do things differently. You need to be different, be more focused and be more out there. To accomplish this, you need to first start with changing your mindset.

People are conditioned to think that they need to find a job, any job. That they need to find and apply to many jobs and hope that one of these applications results in an interview. Well that thinking is probably what got you to where you are today, still unemployed and still searching. So if you want to find the job you really want, at the place you really want to work for, at the salary you really want, you need to change your way of thinking. You need to recalculate your job search.

There is a mathematical formula you need to learn in order to conduct a successful job search resulting in landing your ideal job:

Job Search = Marketing + Sales

Your job search consists of two main activities, marketing and sales. It does not matter whether you are in sales, a management executive, an administrative assistant, a factory worker, or any other title. The formula is still the same.

As I studied marketing and sales and as I started coaching more and more job seekers, I realized how a job search follows exactly the same process as sales. When selling a product, you market the product to find customers, then sell them on the benefits and hopefully get them to buy.

In a job search, you follow the same process. You market yourself to get an interview, then sell yourself during the interview to get a job offer.

So let's look at that math formula again with more detail:

Job Search = Marketing (networking, resumes) + Sales (interviewing, negotiations).

Marketing is all of the activities you do in order to get the job interview. Sales is the interviewing process and hopefully getting a job offer where you can then negotiate the particulars of the offer.

From this point forward, we are going to concentrate on those two main activities in order to get you the job you want. It is vitally important that you get on board with this idea of marketing and sales. This is especially true if you have never done any kind of marketing or sales in your career. This is the time to start.

Don't worry. I'll take you through the highlights of these activities. This is not a detailed step-by-step guide but a high-level guide to the activities you need to do. The first half of this book is focused on the marketing aspects to getting hired. The second half of the book is focused on the sales process to getting hired.

I have three pieces of advice that I give all of my coaching clients. These three things alone will make a world of difference in you, your attitude and your success in your job search.

1. Study and learn all you can about marketing and sales. The process of marketing and selling a product or service are identical to the process of finding and getting hired.
2. Take a public speaking course. Your ability to communicate effectively and persuade others is going to be a major key to winning your next job and moving up the career ladder.
3. Study and learn all you can about your industry. You want to be seen as the expert when you go in for an interview.

Continue to do these three things even after you land your dream job. They will help you tremendously to keep advancing your career - that I can guarantee.

STEP TWO – Finding a Job

"The one piece of advice I can give you is, do what turns you on. Do something that if you had all the money in the world, you'd still be doing it. You've got to have a reason to jump out of bed in the morning."
--Warren Buffet

Chapter Eight

Marketing Yourself

"Without promotion something terrible happens...nothing."
--P.T. Barnum

Your most important task of your job search is marketing yourself. Just like any other business, without marketing you will get no customers. Marketing is what attracts clients to your store, your website, your place of business where you can then begin to sell them on your product.

The same holds true for the job search process. Marketing is what will get your potential employer interested enough in you to invite you in for an interview, where you can then proceed to sell them that you are the solution to their situation.

So this is the first mindset you need to change. You are no longer a job seeker trying to find a job. You are not one of the millions of job seekers out there who endlessly sends out resumes with the hope that someone will notice you.

You are a valuable product and you should not sell yourself to just anybody. You are going to sell your experience, your knowledge and your time to the company that best fits you. You will no longer be begging for a job, you will be finding out who has a problem that you can resolve.

Every hiring manager and every company with a position to fill has a problem they need to resolve. Some advertise what that problem is by posting a job opening. This is great because you don't have to research what the problem is, you just have to research how to best solve it.

Other companies don't advertise it. This is the hidden job market you always hear about. This situation takes more effort because you have to find this out through your marketing efforts. But, the rewards are greater: a better position, better working conditions and a better salary.

Like any good marketing effort, you will need an advertisement brochure: your resume. In a traditional job search, the resume is your primary marketing tool. It is what you are going to deposit in an electronic file on somebody's hard drive.

But you will be taking a non-traditional approach to your job search. In this method, a resume is still necessary but it will not be your primary marketing tool. That task is left to a higher intelligence than a computer. It is left to you. You are going to be the primary person marketing yourself to your future employer, and the primary tool you will be using is your voice. If you want to get the job you want, at the company you want to work for, at the salary you want, you need to use your voice. You need to be talking to people. You need to get up and out of the house and start meeting people.

Just like any great salesperson, you cannot wait for your customers to come to you. You need to seek them out. You need to research and develop the contacts necessary to find the customer who has a problem that you can resolve.

I know it sounds daunting, and might be a little uncomfortable but don't worry. By following the suggestions and procedures outlined in this book, you will get through it. Actually we will get through this together. You made an investment in this book so I will help you along. If you need more help than what's in this book, you can get in touch with me to help you with some personal coaching.

Target Marketing

In order to start your marketing efforts, you need to fully understand the concept of target marketing, sometimes referred to as niche marketing. You can research it on the Internet, but a basic summary of a target market is a group of customers who share some common demographics, that a company focuses their marketing efforts to.

Target marketing is what all successful companies use to develop their marketing strategies. For example, luxury car manufacturers target their marketing to a group of people whose demographics are over thirty-five, successful with a high income. They would not market to a younger crowd.

Companies know that marketing costs time and money and they want to get the best ROI (return on investment) they can. If they tried to market to everyone they would go broke. So as these companies target a certain group of people to focus their marketing efforts, so should you as a job hunter.

The worst thing a job hunter can do is market to everyone, applying for countless jobs, sending out hundreds of resumes in the hopes that someone will call them. This is why a lot of job seekers feel like their search is hopeless, that all they do is send out resume after resume and get no response. That is because they are marketing to everyone, instead of a select group of companies. Companies that actually might buy what they are selling.

So as a job seeker you must focus your time, energy and money on only those companies that have a need for your specific product – which are your specific skills and experience. When you start only marketing to those companies you will see a dramatic rise in the results of your efforts, and you'll start to feel better and more confident.

Since you have now gone through the exercise in the previous chapter of determining what jobs you really want to do and what positions you really want to have, you now need to identify what companies will fit your particular criteria. Remember, you have a unique set of skills. Don't sell them to just anybody.

Chapter Nine

Your Marketing Message

"A person can have the greatest idea in the world – completely different and novel – but if that person can't convince enough other people, it doesn't matter"
--Gregory Berns

Before you can begin any kind of marketing, you have to have a message. A marketing message has several purposes. It is used as a conversation starter, tells the listener who you are and what you can do, answers the question "Why should I talk to you?" and informs the listener of why they should continue to talk to you. Your message is important because you will be using this through every step of the job search process that is detailed in this book.

Like any good business your marketing message is critical to the success of your job search/marketing campaign. It should conjure up an exciting picture in your listeners mind. Think of some of the more unique marketing messages you may have heard through the years:

Miller Lite – Tastes Great, Less Filling
BMW – The Ultimate Driving Machine
Nike – Just Do It
Dairy – Got Milk?

Notice something about these marketing messages? They are all short and sweet. And that's what your marketing message should be -- short and sweet.

I am not a marketing message expert but I've picked up a lot of knowledge and information by studying sales and marketing. If you really want to understand how to craft a great marketing message and make yours one of the best, you need to invest some time and study sales and marketing yourself. Especially if you are a novice in the world of sales and marketing, especially business-to-business selling.

As I've mentioned earlier, the job search process exactly follows the sales process:

Sales Process	*Job Search*
Prospecting	Job ads
Leads & referrals	Networking
Marketing/advertising	Personal message
Sales meeting/presentations	Interviewing
Closing the sale	Getting the job

Do you see how the two fit together?

You may have heard about the concept of developing an elevator speech. This is one of those concepts foreign to job seekers and one that many have a very difficult time developing. That is because the elevator speech was designed by hard-core salesmen back in the days of door-to-door sales. The elevator speech no longer works in today's world of sales and it definitely won't work in your job search.

So why do so many people still try to teach this outdated concept to new unsuspecting job seekers? Maybe because they don't know any other way either. Let's just lose the term elevator speech altogether from this point forward. Instead, use the term marketing message. This will help you keep it in the right frame of mind and focus on what you need to develop and say.

Developing your marketing message

Ideally, you should have a couple of these prepared and ready to go because there is not one universal message that will work in all situations. What you say at one networking group will not be the same as for another, nor should it be the same message you would say when introduced to a prospective employer.

I've sat through endless presentations from other people who go on and on about putting together a thirty second to one minute introduction speech. This is way too long. In this day and age, you need to be much more precise and focused. You have about fifteen seconds to catch someone's attention and gain their interest enough to carry on the conversation.

And that's really what your marketing message should be about, starting a conversation. You don't want to try and spit out your entire resume in thirty seconds, you want to give them enough information to get them intrigued and ask you a question back.

Let me give you an example:

Person: "So what do you do?"

Me: "I work closely with my clients to help them achieve the results they want in the shortest time possible."

Person: "Really? Tell me more."

Me: "Well I coach them through focusing their efforts on the tasks that give them the greatest return of their investment of time, so that they can get the job they really want."

This is just a brief example of a start to a more in-depth conversation, where the two parties can continue to ask questions of each other to gain more information.

Here are three points you want to include in the first fifteen seconds of your opening message.

1. Tell the listener who you are
2. Explain what value you bring
3. Get them to want to hear more

Developing a short introductory message about yourself isn't easy. To help you start developing this message, here are some questions you can ask yourself:

- What do you do well?
- What do you do that is unique?
- What problems can you solve?
- What can you do better, faster, more accurately?
- What do your customers, coworkers, supervisors say about you?
- What is your niche?
- What is your personality?
- What value do you bring?

When I talk about value, I'm referring to the impact you have on an organization. Value could be monetary in the form of revenue or savings, it could be the management you bring, it could be your work ethic or the quality of the work you produce. It is important to state your message with an intrinsic value to it because if it has no value, it has no worth.

Now as I've said before, writing this message could prove challenging to some of you. So let me give you a helpful hint in writing this message - get someone else to write it for you. We often write and say things from our viewpoint, when in fact we should be writing them from the listener's viewpoint. It's about what the listener wants to hear.

People sometimes find it extremely difficult to talk about themselves. We tend to undervalue our self-worth and minimize our accomplishments.

By getting another person to write some information about you, it will be a lot easier to take that information and formulate a clear message from another person's viewpoint. So find someone who knows you and the work you do and ask them to help you write this message. Here are some people you might think about; family members, friends, neighbors, co-workers, networking contacts, old bosses, hiring managers, sales or marketing professionals.

If you're still stuck on writing this message, there is another way you can go about accomplishing it, tell a story. Put together a simple story, around thirty seconds or less, about what you do and why you want to be in this industry.

Here is an example of a short story I put together to introduce myself to prospective employers and new networking contacts back in my job search days:

"From my first job bagging groceries, to being a field engineer, to managing a service organization and finally running my own business, I have been providing services to my customers. Nothing makes me feel better at the end of the day than knowing that I was able to make someone's day a little better by resolving their issue with empathy and a little bit of humor. Through the years, I have experienced many difficult situations and acquired many stories on how I resolved these issues. I would love to share some of these with you."

This story also works great when you're asked that infamous interview question, "Tell me about yourself." (See Chapter Nineteen) When using it for this purpose, you will want to modify it so that it relates in some manner to the company or their industry, or the position you're applying for.

Chapter Ten

Networking

"The richest people in the world look for and build networks, everyone else looks for work."
--Robert Kiyosaki

Networking, now there's a scary word. It causes grown men and women to sweat, run for cover and look under their beds at night in case there is a networker hiding under there. It's scary because for a lot of people it is an uncomfortable activity. Talking to total strangers about your needs and how they can help you can be intimidating, but it doesn't have to be.

There is an awful lot of confusion out there about networking. Most of it is wrong. At least from what I've seen and read, and witnessed by listening to dozens of "experts" who have not done a minute of networking in their lives but feel compelled nonetheless to teach others how to do it.

I will clear this up for you so that you will not only no longer be afraid of networking, but will actually come to enjoy it. Let me first start by setting the record straight about what networking is not about.

Networking is not: attending a job club, finding contacts at a company, filling out your LinkedIn profile, spending hours on Facebook, getting leads on job openings or any other activity that resembles anything in this list. These are all research and information gathering activities.

Networking is truly all about building relationships. Isn't that better? The word relationships may scare some of us guys, and some people may believe that women are better at building relationships than men are.

But in actuality men are just as good at building relationships. We just do it differently. While women build relationships by talking to each other and baring their feelings and souls, guys build relationships by helping their buddy restore that 1963 Chevy. You do it by loaning your neighbor your favorite power tool, or by watching the game at the bar. You just didn't realize you were doing it.

Back to the task at hand. I'm assuming that at this time, you've already gone through your close list of friends, family and contacts in your job search. (You have told everyone and enlisted their help by now haven't you? Right?) If that is the case, or if you simply want to build your list of contacts, you'll need to start networking with strangers.

It's not that bad. If an introvert like me can do it, you can too. Introverts can network. In fact, they make some of the best networkers. Because networking is not about you, it's all about the other person.

Now some of you might be saying "C'mon Tom. If networking isn't about me, why the heck should I be doing it?"

Allow me to explain. The reason most people hate going to networking events is they don't want this scenario to be played out:

You walk into a room full of people at a networking event, strangers mostly, people you have never met before.

You fill out your little stick-on name tag and attach it to your clothing. (You do know to put it on your right side and not your left side right?)

Then someone you have never seen before comes up and says "Hey, how're you doing? My names Bob Wisenheimer and I'm in sales. I can sell anything and everything. Been doing it for 15 years. I'm looking for a job selling ice cubes to Eskimos. Know anybody at any of those companies? No, well it's been nice talking to you. See you around."

Yeah, I would stay away too. But it doesn't have to be that way. In fact, there is a better way. It's what I use to network and it's a process I call S-M-A-R-T Networking.

S = Strategy - You need to have a plan before you go to any networking event. You need to identify who you want to have follow-up conversations with. When I go to a networking event, my plan is to come away with three people I want to follow-up with. No need to put any more pressure on myself. Three people will do. If I come away with more, that's great, but my goal is three people.

M = Make conversation - That's all you're really trying to do, make conversation with someone to find out about them, to give them a little bit of information about yourself. Most importantly, find out how you can help them.

A = Ask questions - That's how you get the conversation going. Ask them questions. What do they do? What are they looking for? How can you help? Don't worry if they don't ask questions about you. Most people will but some won't. Don't worry. Your goal is to see how many people you can help.

R = Respect - Respect other people's time and feelings. Don't bore them with an endless diatribe about how your last company screwed you or how you've sent out thousands of resumes and no one gets back to you. In other words don't be negative.

T = Thanks - Thank everyone for giving you time. Thank them for telling you about themselves and listening to your story, whether or not they can help you. Thank the hosts of the event.

So to get back to my earlier point, networking is about building new relationships. The easiest way to do that is to focus on the other person. When you do that, they will in turn focus on you.

You are also there to help others out. That should be your primary focus. Again, by focusing on helping others, you will also be helping to build a relationship for the future.

"The true measure of a person is how they treat someone who can do them absolutely no good."
--Ann Landers

Don't come to a networking session and expect to walk away with five solid job leads. It doesn't work that way. You may get some ideas on where to look for jobs, but as far as walking away with that coveted "I'll pass your resume on to my boss," well as they say in New Jersey, "Fuggedaboutit."

No one, and I mean no one, is going to walk your resume into their boss's office upon meeting you for a few minutes, at least, no one that you would want to anyway.

On an average, it takes at least three meetings for someone that you just met to get to know enough about you to even think about that. That's why it is so important to find those three people that you want to network further with. Take them out for coffee or offer to buy them lunch.

Get to know them and give them a chance to get to know you.

Even then, the important thing about networking is to just keep looking for information. You can't just come out and ask someone to walk their resume in, they need to know you enough to be able to do that. So the basis for all this networking is to keep getting information and asking for advice. That is why it is so important to use your first-level contacts to introduce you to someone. That introduction from someone they trust can speed up the process.

The key thing about networking is to always, and I mean always, have a positive attitude. You cannot effectively network with a crummy attitude.

Everyone at a job networking event is in the same boat. They have all lost their jobs. So no one wants to hear you complain about how you lost your job, how long you've been out, how the economy sucks, how nobody gets back to you. Keep it positive. Keep your chin up and be cheerful. It'll warm up the people you are meeting.

I've gone to a lot of job networking events and a lot of business networking events. And I can tell you from experience, the major difference between the two is the attitude of the people you meet. Always be cheerful, positive, friendly and polite.

Don't stop networking when you get that new job. Odds are pretty good that some day in the not-so-distant future, you will be once again in this position. Keep on networking so that when the time comes, your network will already be in place, ready to take action.

The Power of Three

Attending a networking event will be a more pleasurable experience if you stop putting so much pressure on yourself. Some people think they have to meet everyone, collect all of their business cards and then follow-up with them all. This is not a good formula for success at networking.

What really works well is to focus on finding only three people. You may find more but only set a goal of finding three people. Three people that you believe you can help the most, have something in common and that you can easily carry on a conversation with. When you find these three people, contact them afterwards and setup a time to meet for coffee. Offer to buy and find a location easily accessible to both of you.

What you want to accomplish at this meeting is to get to know them better and discover how you can best help them in their endeavors. It is important that the emphasis be on them and not on you. Nobody wants to get an invitation to meet so that you can tell them how they can help you.

During the normal mode of conversation, the focus will hopefully get around to you. This will be your opportunity to talk about yourself and your needs. Hopefully at the end of this meeting you would have both come away with more information about the other person and discovered ways in which to help. Setup a time to meet again or to talk on the phone to continue this conversation further.

Do this with each of the three people you have met at that networking event. The end goal of this is to hopefully have these three people introduce you to three people that they know, etc.

By focusing on only meeting three people you will, by a simple mathematical formula, end up meeting more people in the future. Concentrating on three people allows you to narrow down the field making it more manageable and more direct.

Chapter Eleven

Volunteering

"It isn't just what you know, and it isn't just who you know. It's actually who you know, who knows you, and what you do for a living."
--Bob Burg

I could not talk about networking without mentioning the greatest networking of all and that is volunteering, which is really networking in disguise. It is the absolute best form of networking you can do while you are looking for a job, when you are employed, and when you are looking for your next job.

Have you ever seen a resume for the CEO of a company? No? Well neither have I. And I would bet a lot of other people have not either. But you will see their picture in the paper at some charity event or another. And you can bet, they know a lot of people. You will see the movers and the shakers in newspapers, industry magazines, and on television.

There are many different ways to volunteer your time and services. And every single one of them will pay you back dividends in unimaginable ways. Volunteering is so important in the job hunting process because you get an opportunity to work side-by-side with someone else. And that someone else might just be one of those aforementioned CEO's, or their sister, aunt, neighbor or employed at a company you want to work for.

While you are working side-by-side with these people, you start to form a relationship with them. And while you are working with them, they get to know you, the kind of work you do and the kind of person you are. That is the best way to get into your next position. So even if it does not pan out in the short term - think long term. In case you lose your job again or simply want a career change. Let me tell you a short story.

About five years ago, I started volunteering my time as a career coach at a job club run by a local church. I was not a member of this church but they ran an announcement in the local paper about starting this job club and needing volunteers.

I wasn't doing much with my time and I knew a thing or two about job searching and hiring. So I walked in on a Tuesday before one of their meetings and told them I wanted to volunteer my time. I had never met any of these people before, but they welcomed me with open arms and I got right at it and stated helping the people who needed assistance.

Over the years, I have built great relationships with the other people who volunteered at this job ministry. We know about each other's past and what we are currently doing but most of all, we know the kind of work each of us can do and we know the type of person each one of us are.

And if the need arose, I would not hesitate for a second to walk their resume into someone's office and suggest that they seriously consider this person for a position; or recommend their services to someone else. And I believe they would do the same for me.

If you have never volunteered for anything in your life, it is time to start. This will be a better use of your time than surfing the Internet or watching reruns on TV.

I must caution you on one thing. Do not, I repeat do not, volunteer with the thought process that the only reason you are doing this is to network for a job. Do this because you sincerely want to help people. No matter how bad you have it, there is always someone out there who has it much worse then you. Do this because you want to help them.

The bonus of building a trusted network is something that comes over time. Concentrate on helping someone, being there for them and the organization. Work as hard for the cause or the organization as you would any job you've ever had. The rest will come to you. I guarantee it.

First of all, you need to find an organization to volunteer for. That's the easy part. There are literally hundreds of opportunities out there, but not all may be in your area. Let me point out a few.

National Organizations

There are the usual well know organizations out there: American Red Cross, March of Dimes, Salvation Army, American Cancer Society, Big Brothers, Big Sisters, Habitat For Humanity, Rotary Club, The National Exchange Club, Kiwanis, and Boy and Girl Scouts. You can go to their websites to find a chapter near you.

Besides all of these organizations needing local people to help out, there is another plus to these organizations. Each one has a National Headquarters and maybe even some local offices that employee people to keep them running. You can get a great leg up on your competition when a position opens up, if you are already familiar with the inner workings of that organization.

For example, in my neighboring town, the local chapter of a national service organization holds a gigantic fund-raising event a year. It is a five day festival that includes food vendors, carnivals, major musical acts, (Styx, REO Speedwagon, Lynyrd Skynyrd, etc.), and culminates with one of the largest and best fireworks show around. All of this is coordinated by volunteers of this organization. It takes many volunteers and a lot of dollars to run this event. Do you think helping out with an event such as this could help your chances in finding a job now or in the future?

Trade Associations

Most industries have a trade association. Most associations have some kind of event at least once a year. Contact an association affiliated with your industry and offer to volunteer at their next event. Better: If you can afford it, join that organization. A lot of them offer discounted rates for unemployed people. You'll then be able to attend meetings and get to know people in that industry, employed people. People you want to get to know and who want to get to know you. Plus, these associations have a vested interest in getting and keeping their members employed.

Community Organizations

Local churches, hospitals, villages and park districts are always looking for people to help out. Investigate your local community and help out. Local chambers of commerce sometimes sponsor events needing assistance. The chamber in my town sponsors a 10k race very year and is always looking for volunteers to help run it.

Homeowner associations, libraries, colleges, Parent Teacher Associations, senior citizen centers, fire and police departments. A lot of communities have started emergency management groups made up of volunteers to help out the local fire and police departments during emergencies. Veteran centers and animal shelters are always in need of help.

How about political organizations? There are elections going on somewhere. Do you have a candidate you feel strongly about? Volunteer to help out in their next election. There are plenty opportunities out there, go find one.

While it is a great thing to volunteer your time and help out, you can really scale up your volunteering by taking it a step further. Almost all of these organizations also will have committees of some kind. Volunteer to head up a committee or campaign or step up and hold an office within the organization.

Raise your hand every time an opportunity comes up. Help out the organization at every opportunity that presents itself. Make yourself well known to those in the organization. In life what goes around comes around. Pay it forward and reap the dividends sometime in the future. You'll be helping out others who are in need, and getting a gold star for your efforts.

Other Benefits of Volunteering

Learning new skills – While a lot of companies today do not want to take the time to train their employees, the opposite is true in volunteer organizations. There is always someone who will take the time to train you on your job. Once you are trained and become proficient at a task, you can add this skill to your resume.

Fill in gaps on your resume – It is taking months and sometimes years to find a job today. Volunteering is a great way to fill in that void on your resume. And yes, hiring managers will take this into consideration.

Leadership – By taking on a leadership role in a volunteer organization, you can acquire managerial skills you may not get in any other job. Managing people in a volunteer organization is different than managing them in a corporate environment. For one thing, you really have no power over them since they are a volunteer. Getting them all moving in the right direction takes exceptional persuasive management skills. Again, this is looked upon favorably by hiring managers.

Making a difference – This is without a doubt the best benefit of volunteering, knowing that in some way your efforts are making a difference in someone else's life, someone who is desperately needing it. There is no better feeling in the world then when I come home from my volunteer work and realize that one little thing I did that day, may help another person get closer to their goal.

Feeling good about yourself – This is probably the second best benefit of volunteering. You get a really great feeling from helping others. It makes you feel alive, needed and cherished, things that can naturally go away when you've been downsized and are looking for employment.

"It is one of the most beautiful compensations in life....that no man can sincerely try to help another without helping himself."
--Ralph Waldo Emerson

Chapter Twelve

Job Boards and Job Fairs

"Insanity is doing the same thing, over and over again, but expecting different results."
--Albert Einstein

I call all of these time wasters because the possibility of you finding your perfect job through them is pretty slim. The reason for this is just the sheer number of job applicants you will be competing against. With one simple click of a button, a thousand job seekers could be applying for the same job you are. And going to a job fair usually requires standing in a long line waiting to get in and waiting to talk to a recruiter. Still, they can be useful in doing research.

Job Boards

While some people have found a job and got hired by applying through Internet job boards, they are the vehicle that provides the lowest percentage of you landing your ideal job. If you want to spend your time exploring job boards then go ahead.

But they are useful in some way and that way is research. Let's walk through some examples of how to use these resources to find information:

Researching a career: If you are looking at changing careers, job boards are a great tool to identify skills you may need. Just search for the particular position to get a snapshot of many different job listings and what skills they are looking for. Then by doing you own assessment, identify those skills you already have and which ones you need to acquire.

Finding companies in your target industry: By using the search function, you can find companies that are in the industry you are looking in. For example, let's say you are interested in an accounting job. Besides searching for jobs in accounting, you can enter a search for telecommunications. Find companies that have listings under that category. Use this information to do further research on the companies you found there. Odds are, there may be quite a few that you never heard of before. Also, you may find companies that are headquartered out of state that you may not have thought of.

Researching a target company: Again by using the search function you can enter your target company name and find different information about the company or you can peruse openings that may be posted even if your particular position is not listed. By reading these listings, you can gain a sense of what they are looking for and the company culture.

Gathering competitive information: Do a search for companies that are competitors of your target companies or a company that you are applying to or interviewing with. Find listings from those companies to gather information on them to use for your knowledge.

Now as much as I know from personal experience that these job boards are a waste of time, I have known people who have gotten interviews from them and even hired. But again, your odds of getting a job through these are minimal at best just because of the sheer number of applicants. A recent study showed that on one major job aboard alone, there were seventy million stored resumes and more than one million job postings.

But if you want to use them for something other than research, here are some pointers:

First, do not log onto job boards during your prime working time, log on late at night when there's nothing better to do.

Second, if you find a job that is interesting to you, go to the company's website. If the job is posted there, apply for it on their website. If it is not posted there, before you waste any time building a resume, call the company. Ask for the HR department and inquire if that position is still open. If it is, ask the person on the phone which is the best way to apply.

Lastly, do not post your resume on these job boards with any personal information on it. You don't want someone to download your resume and forward it without your permission.

Job Fairs

In my own personal experience, most of the job fairs I have been to have turned into a total bust. In all my years of coaching, I have not met a single person who has gotten a job from a career fair.

As with job boards, you are dealing with a large volume of job applicants all looking to apply for the same jobs you are. You take time out from more useful activities, get all dressed up, walk into a crowded hot room, stand in long lines waiting your turn to talk to one of the recruiters who after all that, tell you to go to their company website and apply on line.

It has also been my direct observation that most of the companies attending these job fairs are advertising lower level and entry level positions. If this is the type of position you are looking for, then by all means feel free to attend one near you. But if you are looking to land your ideal job, then let me suggest a couple of ways you can use job fairs to assist in your job search:

Research: You can use them to find companies. You might find a company that eluded your initial target list by researching the Internet, or was just small enough to fall under your radar scope.

Find open positions. Not every company lists all openings at their job fair booths. They might be there to hire for certain positions, like entry level or customer service. You can spend a few minutes talking to the recruiters about other positions.

You can spend time gathering information on the company from the material they have available; or by just talking to the people manning the booth. I've found most are very open with giving information about their company. I've even gotten the names of hiring managers this way. But you just can't come out and ask for them. You have to show genuine interest in the company by asking questions and giving some information about yourself.

You can also pick up some information on competitors of a company you are interested in.

Networking: Anytime you can go to an event where there are lots of other people around is an opportunity to network that you should not pass up.

Again, you can network with the people who are manning the job fair booths. Most of these people have a vested interest in finding quality people for their company. Your aim is not to get involved in a long conversation with them at the fair, but get their contact information and ask if it is okay to follow up with them in a couple of days to find out more about the company. Then go home and send them an email that day or the next. Remind them that you met them at the ____ Job Fair and that you asked about following up with them. Then suggest some times to get together for a phone conversation.

Meet other job seekers. Your opportunity here is to offer information to other job seekers. Everyone there is in the same boat as you, trying to find a job. Strike up conversations with those waiting in line with you, someone who is walking around, getting refreshments, or someone who just looks like they need someone to talk to. As with all networking events, your goal is to find the three people you most want to have a longer follow-up conversation with.

Hint: Don't try to network with recruiters when their booth is crowded and there is a line waiting. Walk around a little more and wait until there is a lull in the action.

Chapter Thirteen

Social Media, Email and Personal Websites

"Everything you post on social media impacts your personal brand. How do you want to be known?"
--Lisa Howard Horn

If you use them wisely, social media , email and websites can play a big part in your job search. In fact if you don't use them wisely you're almost better off not using them at all.

Social Media (LinkedIn, Facebook, Twitter)

I am admittedly not an expert on social media. There are a lot of experts out there who can give you much more detailed information than I can on how to use this tool. Experts such as Mari Smith (www.marismith.com) or Melonie Dodaro (www.topdogsocialmedia.com).

But I have picked up some tidbits of knowledge on the subject from my own experience with them, by learning about them, and through my coaching practice.

The number one rule to remember about Social Media and your job search is this:

Be careful what you put out there!

There is an old adage about not mixing your professional life with your business life. And as the use of social media continues to gain in popularity, this sometimes becomes harder and harder to do. Workmates, bosses and customers become friends on social media. We invite more and more people into our social media world in that constant quest to have the most connections, which could be a detriment to you if you are embroiled in a career search. My word of caution is this: if you post something somewhere, it is almost a 100% guaranteed fact that someone somehow, is going to find it, whether directly or indirectly.

But there is a way to use these tools in your job search while still maintaining contact with your network.

LinkedIn

Since the object of this book is to scale up your job search and get you employed quickly, LinkedIn is going to be your primary tool as it is a professional networking site. Using LinkedIn wisely can be one of the best ways to find connections to companies you have an interest in.

The first thing you want to do on LinkedIn is create your profile and make it as complete as possible. Fill out your prior job positions going as far back as you think is useful with relevant job information. Your profile information should include the company name, your title and a brief description of the work you did there. This is not the place to enter all the information from your resume.

Your LinkedIn photo

Even I have a photo on my LinkedIn profile. So if my mug can be on LinkedIn, so can yours. This is a very important step that a lot of members skip. I have yet to hear a great answer from anyone on why they don't have a picture. But there are a couple of good reasons to have one:

First, it helps people to connect to you. How many times have you searched for someone on LinkedIn only to find there are twenty people with the same name? It's happened to me a lot. If I know the person closely, I can usually scan their profile and determine which Bobby Jones is my friend. But if I just met you at an event, I probably won't know enough about you to determine which Gina Smith is the one I met yesterday. Having a photo will help someone remember who you are.

Second, it just completes your profile. It shows that you are a human being and not some electronic social media bot.

Hints on your photo

- This is a professional networking site. Don't use the picture of you doing a cannonball at last year's family reunion. Post a nice subtle professional headshot in a business suit or at the least, business casual clothing. Make sure you smile and your photo has a nice subtle background.
- Don't include anyone else in the picture but you.
- Don't post a computer generated avatar of yourself. People hire humans not computers.

67

Connecting to others

Once you have completed your profile, you can then start connecting with others and adding them to your list. This is the benefit of being on LinkedIn, the connections. Use them wisely. Start with people you already know who are on LinkedIn and send them an invitation to connect with you.

Tip: When requesting to connect with someone, do not, I repeat do not, just use the generic LinkedIn message. Customize it in some way. Especially if it is not a close connection or if it is someone you found in a group or at a networking event. Tell them how you know them or why they should connect to you.

LinkedIn will automatically start suggesting people you can connect with if you want to. People will also start finding you as well and will start sending you invitations to connect, accept these as well.

Tip: Be careful of who you connect with, especially if you don't know the person because your profile will show who your connections are. You want your connections to be as professional as you are.

People sometimes have the wrong perception of connections on LinkedIn and believe that you need to have hundreds of connections. It's not the quantity of connections you have, it's the quality of the connections you have.

Here's why you want to keep your connections as close as possible to people you know really well. Let's suppose Stan asks me to introduce him to Sheila because she is the hiring manager for a position at a company he wants to work for. Now think about these two scenarios:

Scenario 1

I know Stan really well, we've worked together in the past and he would be a great fit for that position. But I really don't know Sheila. In fact, I can't even remember how we got connected. So I can take a chance on asking Sheila to talk to Stan, but odds are she won't. So now I have to explain to Stan that I don't really know Sheila. This might be okay on a one time basis, but what if it happens again to another person Stan asks me to introduce him to? If I was Stan, I would question my credibility with all of my connections.

Scenario 2

Brett contacts me for an introduction to Priscilla. I know Priscilla really well, we've been friends ever since we worked together 10 years ago. I just recently connected with Brett because he is in one of the same groups I'm in. Now I'm stuck in another bad scenario. I can take a chance that Brett is okay, and introduce him to Priscilla. If it turns out that Brett is a real loser, I've now just soured my relationship with Priscilla and she will be less likely in the future to talk to anyone I ask her to. Or, I can explain to Brett that I don't know him enough to introduce him to Priscilla. Which may not make Brett feel better, but that can then open up an opportunity to have several conversations with Brett.

So you see, you don't want to risk messing up any of your connections on LinkedIn. I have a standing policy of declining all invitations to connect with people I've never met or never had any interactions with. It keeps my connection list clean and close to the heart.

And introductions are the lifeblood of LinkedIn. It's why people use it in the first place. To get introduced to people they don't know, through a trusted third party. That's the way to get to those hidden jobs and the hiring managers.

Another thing you want to do on your LinkedIn profile is to get recommendations from others. Don't confuse recommendations with endorsements. Recommendations are real, some endorsements are not.

What is a recommendation?

It is a summary of your character, work ethic, skills and personality that is written by someone else. These could be coworkers, past bosses, community leaders, or other people (never use family members) who know you well and can vouch for you and the work you do.

You need to ask your connections for a recommendation. They will then in turn hopefully write a short paragraph about you.

Tip: When asking someone for a recommendation, explain what position you would like them to write about and what skills if necessary. It just helps them get an understanding of what you are looking for.

When you get your recommendation back, you will have a chance to review it before posting it.

Recommendations are just like connections. It is about the quality of the recommendation and not the quantity. Do not over load your profile with too many recommendations; it will look cluttered, unreadable and unbelievable.

What is an endorsement?

Endorsements are a way for you to endorse the skills of your connections and they in turn can endorse your skills. This is how endorsements work. I can click on a connections profile, scroll down to their skills and endorse them for that skill. Likewise your connections can endorse you for your skills.

As with recommendations, it is the quality of your endorsements that count not the quantity. An endorsement by a higher authority is great. An endorsement by your cousin Bertha is not so great.

Whatever you do, please do not endorse someone for a skill that you have no idea if they are good at or not. If you have never worked with someone, how can you endorse any of their work skills? It is really a false endorsement and carries no weight. An endorsement is not a "like" button as it is on Facebook.

Groups

The next thing you want to do is join groups. Only join groups that are professionally interesting to you and that you will get something out of. Then be an active member on these groups. Start discussions on them. Comment on existing discussions. Make sure your comments are always professional, because others can view them and your connections will get updates on them.

Facebook

To use Facebook effectively during your job search there is something you need to do immediately: Clean Up Your Act.

First, get rid of all photos showing you doing all kinds of goofy stuff and all embarrassing posts that could reflect badly on you. Second, set your privacy settings to friends only and don't invite your potential boss into your Facebook world.

Once you have done this parsing, it is time to put your Facebook account to good use in finding your next job. The first use of this tool should be to make use of your current network of friends. Now is the time to tell them about your job search. Let them know what is going on and how they can help. Tell them about the work you do and what you are looking for. Don't ask them if they know of anyone who is hiring, this puts them on the spot. Gently keep them in the loop by posting updates.

Little by little, ask them for their help in getting connected to someone at XYZ company, or see if they know someone in the industry you are interested in. Make it clear that you just want to learn something from these people and that you are not actually looking for a position there, even if there is one open. You don't want your contacts to be wary of passing you information on someone. You want to keep them engaged in just helping you find information. This is a lot easier then asking someone to get you a job.

Once you have your army looking out for you, the other use of Facebook is to start following companies you are interested in. This is a great way to get information on these companies. You might be able to get additional information that you can use in your resume, cover letter and in your interview. Follow and "like' their Facebook pages. Post interesting and professional comments on them because in most cases, someone is monitoring them.

Twitter

Okay I will admit I have not as yet used Twitter myself. But I will be actively using Twitter as a way to promote my business in the not too distant future. But I have read a lot of articles and listened to some webinars on using Twitter not only to promote a business but how to effectively use it in a job search.

Based on the what I have learned and researched so far, here are some good uses of Twitter:

Follow companies: Find companies that you are interested in working for and start following them. This is another good way of gathering information on them.

Follow industry leaders: Find people in your industry or occupation that are knowledgeable and are good sources of information. This is especially useful if you are trying to break into new industries.

Follow other sites: College alumni offices, career centers, coaches, journalists and trade magazines. All of these will help in painting a better picture of you to the world.

Retweet: When some great information gets out on one of your companies or experts, retweet it. It's a way of showing interest and gets you noticed along the way.

Post: Tweet some information about a company or about a great article you just read. Make sure it is of a professional nature and pertinent to the companies and industries you are following.

Ask questions: Ask a question about a company or of one of those industry experts. This leads to natural follow-up conversations which could be your "in" to that company.

Other notes on Social Media

Make sure the content you are posting is meaningful and focused to your job search. Don't just blast out an article, include your own comments.

Always be upbeat and positive. Never be negative or voice criticism about past bosses, companies or bad relationships. Make positive suggestions on how something can be improved.

Don't spend all your time on social media. You don't want to give the impression that you spend your whole day on it. Check it a couple of times a day, maybe in the morning and in the evening, just as you would if you were employed. If you are still employed, don't post on social media during working hours. You don't want your potential employer to get the idea that you will do that at their place also.

Don't get too personal or use profanity. Make sure to check your spelling and use emoticons wisely. Not everyone on the receiving end will interpret them in the way you meant.

Use social media to build your "brand" in a professional manner. Your future employer may be watching and following you.

Email

Email is an effective tool when job searching. If fact, it is probably one of the most used tools during your job search encompassing everything from sending in resumes, making contact with people, setting up networking meetings and interviews.

But like everything else, it can be a detriment if not used correctly. Here are some helpful hints to keep you on the straight-and-narrow:

1. Get yourself a professional email address. While honeybuns123@xyz.com might be cute for your friends and family, it is a sure fire killer during a job hunt. Open a new email account with a professional address. yourname@xyz.com or some derivative of that. Use modern and up-to-date email providers.

2. Don't send unsolicited attachments. This is a great way for your email to wind up in a spam filter, especially if it is sent to someone who does not know you. In fact, most receivers of this kind of email automatically delete them without opening them. Paste your resume into the body of

the email and offer to send a formatted document if requested.

3. Use SPELL CHECK! Nothing will show your unprofessionalism as quickly or as surely as having typos in your email. But don't put all your trust into spell check, have someone else proofread it as an added level of checking for spelling, grammar and the proper use of words. (There, they're, their for example).

4. This is not a text message. No OMG's or LOL's or any of those other nomenclatures everyone likes to text. Type out the whole word.

Misspelled words and incorrect grammar usage in resumes and email is one of the key things that companies look for and will use to eliminate you from consideration. Don't risk the opportunity by skipping this simple step.

Personal Website

The Internet is the job seekers most useful tool. Not only can you use it to research companies and get information, you can use it to promote and market yourself as well, with your own personal website.

Now I know what you're probably thinking "How the heck am I going to afford a website?" Well, you can actually get a website for as little as $20. This should about cover the cost of your domain name for a year. Add a few more dollars for hosting and you're all set. There are many deals out there for names and hosting and you don't need anything really extravagant at this point.

I've dabbled in creating my own website and if I could do it you could probably do it too. There are free templates you can use to create your website easily and in less than a day. There are online tutorials and articles out there about creating one.

You can take a course at a community college, or even better, find a student at a college who would create one for you for a $100 or so. You can find people on the Internet who will build you one for even less than that.

So I am not going to go through any detail on creating a website, but I will step through what you could and should do on your website, and some things you shouldn't do.

Here are the basic things you would want to have on your website:

- A contact me page
- A bio of your work experience
- An About Me page (not work history, but a little bit about you personally. Your values, work ethic, mission statement and what value you will bring to an employer).
- A blog page
- A page to upload movies and pictures of yourself, projects you worked on, things you built at other companies and other professional documentation that is not copyrighted and is your own work product.

Why a blog? I'm glad you asked. You can use your blog to publish your own articles about anything. I would again keep it professional and focused on your field. So write your own thoughts about your work. Reference other blog posts that you thought were inspirational or though producing about your industry.

Talk about companies you are interested in and the kind of work they do. Talk about business or technology issues. You don't have to go hog wild on this and post something hourly, once a week is a good reference to start with to keep you active.

Videos are another great device to use in your job search marketing. You don't have to go out and spend hundreds of dollars on video and audio equipment. You can record these with a standard camcorder or even your smartphone. Just make sure Junior is not crying or the dog is not barking in the background when you record it. Keep it professional and explain your own thought and ideas.

Video also gives anyone who visits your website a chance to see the real you, to get to know your personality and what you are about. And the cool thing is, video can be re-recorded. So if you mess up, you get as many second chances as you need. The quality of the video is not as important as the content and how you present yourself. Your final edit should not have any stumbles and should be concise and have a point.

So here's an idea, why not take some of those pesky interview questions, and record your answers on video? Or have someone interview you and post that interview. Yes, everyone will know it was rehearsed but so what? This is after all a marketing video.

Always keep in mind that the purpose of this website it to promote yourself as a professional in order to get a new job. While there are an endless number of things you can do on your own website to promote yourself, there are some things you should not do:

- Invite comments without moderating them.
- Rant about former bosses, employees or co-workers.
- Cast disparaging comments about companies.
- Be negative in any way. Again, you can suggest changes in a positive way.
- Post anything about religion, politics and sex. (Exception; you can post a column giving your insight on how a recent political event or court ruling may affect your industry. As long as you don't badmouth the party or politician involved.)

This is also a great way for you to learn new skills and show off your technology prowess. So there you have it, some insight into using a website to market yourself. Have fun with it and be creative.

Note: Your website should be an additional tool for you to use in your job search. It should not be a substitute for getting out and networking, applying for jobs and interviewing. You should also not ask a prospective employer to go to your website to download your resume, because your resume should be customized to each job you apply for.

Chapter Fourteen

Resumes

"You have to learn the rules of the game. And then you have to play better than anyone else."
--Albert Einstein

This chapter is not going to show you all of the details about writing a resume. There is an over-abundance of information on the Internet, in your library or in your local book store on how to write a resume. Take some time and read up on it. What I am going to show you is my perspective on what a hiring manager looks for on a resume.

Some job seekers believe that their resume is the number one tool that will get them a job. In fact, they depend on it so much that they will invest hundreds of dollars to get a resume professionally written.

That's a great tactic to take if you are a) bad at writing or b) don't care what job you get. The problem with a professionally written resume is this: you will only get one resume from them. If you want another resume, you will need to pay them again for each new resume you want. Why do you need more than one resume? Read the following section on writing a resume to get the answer.

Before you start to put together a resume, you need to understand that the only purpose of a resume is to get an interview. There is no other use for it. In fact, once you are in the interview stage, a resume becomes something to take notes on, a piece of reference material. Some hiring managers don't even bring one to an interview. How does that sit with all your hard work and expense of putting one together?

Your resume is a marketing tool you to get an interview. It is necessary because at some point in time, someone is going to request one from you. So you might as well take the time to prepare one correctly.

Writing your resume

There are basically two ways to write a resume; the right way and the wrong way.

The wrong way is to put together a generic resume that looks like any other resume you can pull off of the Internet. It is all about you and your accomplishments, your work history, and your education. It is the type of resume you will get from one of those expensive resume writers. I know, I paid for one myself.

The right way is to write a resume that is focused on the company, the hiring manager, and the problems they are facing that you can resolve. It answers the main questions in the hiring manager's mind: "Why should I hire you?"

Your resume needs to connect the dots in the hiring manager's mind so that there is no question that you can do the job, you want the job and you are the right person for the job. Do not assume that the hiring manager will make that connection. Remember, this is your marketing brochure. If it is not easy to read, understand or does not clearly paint a picture of who you are and what you can do, then you're ending up in the circular file.

Your resume must also answer another very important question for the hiring manager. That question is; "So What"?

Actually the real question is a little longer; "So what does this mean to me?" "What does all this stuff on your resume mean to me, my team and my organization? How does this make you different or better than other candidates?"

You don't want a hiring manager to try and figure this out for themselves. Most won't take the time and will simply move on to the next resume. And what if they do try and then interpret it wrong? As the author of your resume, you need to take them down the road to where everything meets to a point where they know you are the first person they want to interview.

Getting your resume to this point is not all that difficult, you simply need to avoid making the same mistakes that most job seekers make when writing a resume.

The first mistake is most people write a resume the way that makes sense to them. **They** write a resume that highlights what **they** want to highlight, the accomplishments that **they** are most proud of, and the education that **they** think is important. This is absolutely wrong and will not get you where you want to be, on the top of the pile.

Your resume should be written from the viewpoint of the person reading it, not the person who is writing it. In other words, you need to write so the hiring manager who is reading it can easily understand it. You need to write it in their language which is about their industry, their company and their department. A hiring manager needs to understand how your accomplishments can help her today in her company.

Let's say you are applying for a job at a widget manufacturing company but your experience is in the thingy industry. In order for your accomplishments to make more sense to the hiring manager, you need to change your resume so that your accomplishments make sense to the someone in the widget industry. What you accomplished in one industry does not always have the same effect in another industry.

For example, let's say that you were a salesperson for a company that did fifty million dollars in sales per year, and you brought in one million of that revenue. If you are applying for a job with a company that does five-hundred million in sales and the average salesperson generates ten million in sales, your one million could look small. Instead of dollar amounts, focus on the percentage of sales you brought in, the amount you increased sales by or how much over quota you were. You would use the same process if you were going from the larger company to a smaller company. The large dollar amount in sales you generated might scare a smaller company.

The same would hold true if you saved a company money or increased production. Keep your resume focused on percentages instead of dollar amounts. The hiring manager can calculate the numbers as they apply to their business.

Imagine yourself as the hiring manager reading your resume. What would you most likely want to see? What information would prove to you that that applicant can do the job? You see, the problem is a hiring manager doesn't really care what you think is impressive. They've got a position to fill and the only thing they care about is what you can bring to the table that solves this problem for them.

The second mistake that job seekers make on their resume is including too much information. Here's the thing; your resume should be 100% focused directly on the job and the company you are applying to. That means that only the accomplishments you achieved that directly relate to the job should be on the resume.

There are some assumptions a hiring manager will make when reading your resume. They will assume that you are performing the same basic tasks as anyone would in your position. If you are applying for a customer service job, they will assume that you have the basic skills of a customer service rep; answering phones, handling complaints and entering data. A sales position, they will assume that you know how to prospect, how to forecast and how to sell. You don't need to list these on your resume. They just take up valuable space and make your resume harder to read.

Leave off terms such as team player, hard worker, conscientious, focused, etc. They make your resume generic and boring and take up valuable space. Plus those terms are totally subjective. Your definition of these terms may not match the hiring manager's definition.

Don't list skills that make you the same as everyone else such as proficient in Microsoft Office, email or communications. Just about everyone has these skills and again, they are pretty much assumed that you have them.

A short resume that is totally focused on the requirements of this position is one-hundred times better than a resume that is longer but contains information not relevant to that position.

Master Resume

The key to writing a focused resume is to start with what I call a master resume. Unlike a resume that you will be sending to your future employer, this resume should be as long as you can make it, the longer the better.

Your master resume is a collection of every accomplishment, every skill, every function that you ever had in your career.

Remember that exercise you did to determine the right job for you? Those items you listed in that exercise is a great stating point to build your master resume. Take all of those items and enter them in bullet points in whatever word processing system you use. I find it easier to just enter them all in no particular order at first. Keep adding to the list as you think about them.

Now that you've got all your data entered, create two new files. In one file, organize the skills and accomplishments under the companies under which they occurred. In the second file, organize the skills by category. For example, list all skills and accomplishment that apply to customer service under that heading, list management skills under management, sales skills under sales and so on. It's okay if an accomplishment can be listed under more than one heading, this is just for your use anyway. Once you have all of your skills and accomplishments entered, start adding in education, volunteer work and seminars.

Now you've completed your master resume. It should contain every skill, accomplishment and educational level you've ever accomplished.

This is how you use this master resume: when you are preparing a resume to apply for a job, use this master resume to paste only those items that are pertinent to the job you are applying for. The great thing about the master resume is that you don't have to spend a significant amount of time every time you send out a resume thinking of when and where you had identical skills. They are already there in your master resume. Now you can spend your valuable time rewording the bullet points so that they match exactly to the requirements listed on the job posting.

A second function of this master resume is that when you start building your custom resume for this job, you can easily see which requirements you match up with, (strengths) and which ones you don't (weaknesses). This will help you start to prepare answers to those areas in which you may have a weakness, and help you to really hit home on your strengths.

Resumes should read like a newspaper. When you read a newspaper, what is the first thing that grabs your attention? The headline right? It jumps off of the page and either grabs your interest or not. The first paragraph is a synopsis of the details that will entice one to read the rest of the story, which provides additional details. Now once you start reading, if the column is too long, most people will give up on it or skim through it to read the parts that interest them. The same holds true for your resume.

Your summary at the top is your headline and the equivalent of the first paragraph of a news story. This is what's going to grab the hiring manager's attention and make her decide if she is going to read the rest of it. Then your skills and major accomplishments will entice her to read further and get the rest of the details.

But I will mention it again, everything on your resume should focus on the job for which you are applying.

Sending out a generic resume screams out one single message:

I will take any job and I am too lazy to do enough research on your company to figure out if I am the right person for your company or how I can actually benefit your company

Somewhere in the world of job seeking, an amazing new statistic has been battered about. It's been said that most people scan a resume for fifteen to thirty seconds to determine if you are a candidate. Fifteen to thirty seconds. Someone must have taken a speed-reading course. That's like spending all day cooking a holiday meal, only to have everyone finish eating it in five minutes. So you may spend one to two hours or more developing a resume, only to have someone spend fifteen seconds reading it.

So I did some research on this topic and what I've discovered is that those statistics are mostly for recruiters. Your average corporate or contract recruiter spends an average of fifteen to thirty seconds to glance over your resume. Notice the operative word here is glanced. There is no way anyone can truly read a resume in fifteen to thirty seconds.

Since corporate and contract recruiters are not the hiring manager, when you look at the research on this you realize that the only thing they are looking for in this short period of time is a reason to eliminate you as a candidate. Let me repeat that. THEY ARE LOOKING TO ELIMINATE YOU!!

You want to know why hiring managers cannot find good candidates? You just read it. They are letting someone else make their decisions for them.

That is why it is absolutely imperative that you find a way to get your resume directly to the hiring manager. Hiring managers will spend more time reading over your resume than the average recruiter. And, they can make their own decisions on who might be a good candidate. Even then, you still only have a fifty percent success rate in making the cut.

But a hiring manager will spend a considerable amount of time reading a resume that was forwarded to her *from a trusted source*. Much more than thirty seconds, much, much more. In fact, yours will probably make the "A" list.

Remember, thirty seconds is only enough time to eliminate someone, not to decide if they are a good candidate. Also remember that the purpose of a resume is to get the interview. And you do this by focusing the resume entirely on the job and the company, showing proof that you have the skills to do the job.

Chapter Fifteen

Cover Letters

"To write well, express yourself like the common people, but think like a wise man."
--Aristotle

While a resume shows proof that you can do the job, a cover letter is your opportunity to show how you can do it better than anyone else.

This is one of the most frequent questions I get asked by job seekers; should they include a cover letter with their resume?

While there are some who will say that a cover letter is no longer necessary, that no one reads them anymore, there are some, namely me, who say what does it hurt?

Look at it this way. There are still a lot of hiring managers out there who will read your cover letter. But there are some that won't. The smart play is to include a cover letter with every resume you send out. If the person you are sending it to is expecting one and you don't send one, you're out. If someone doesn't want to read it, they will just flip it over and start reading your resume. But it is better to be on the safe side.

I think this whole don't send a cover letter fad was started by lazy managers and even lazier job applicants.

What better way to get a first opportunity to talk to the hiring manager than with a cover letter?

The cover letter is your opportunity to express your interest in the company and the position. It is an opportunity to tell the hiring manager a little bit about yourself and why you are applying for this job. It is an opportunity for you to peak the hiring manager's interest.

As a hiring manager, I love reading cover letters. I can tell more about a person from their cover letter than I can from their resume. If I had my druthers, I would rather get a two page well written cover letter than a one page so-so resume.

So why are most people so confused and stressed out about writing a cover letter? They have no clue how to write one. You should see some of the cover letters I've read. They are the same ones everyone downloads from the Internet, makes a few changes to, and then sends to me.

Here is how to write a cover letter that will catch a hiring manager's attention.

Your cover letter should be no longer than three to four paragraphs. Don't write a novel and don't give me bullet points. Also, do not just copy information from your resume and paste it into the cover letter. This is redundant and makes for boring reading.

The first paragraph should indicate what job you are applying for. The hiring manager might have multiple job openings. A little help telling them which one you are applying for would be most appreciated.

The second paragraph should tell the hiring manager a little bit about yourself. Nothing too detailed, they don't really care about your childhood or your ailing parents. Tell them a little bit about how you got into your career, or why you are looking to change careers. Make it light and easy to read. Put a lot of your personality into it. You're either a fit or you're not. Don't try to fake it.

In the third paragraph tell the hiring manager what you know about their company and the position. Don't copy and paste from the website or the job description. They most likely know all that stuff. They want to know what you know, or what you perceive it to be. Again, tell them in your own words – especially if you can relate to a problem you can fix.

With the fourth paragraph tell them why you are the best person for this job. Don't over sell yourself, but don't undersell yourself either. Find a happy middle ground.

Do not under any circumstances tell them that you will call them to set up a time to talk. I'm not sure where the notion that this is a great idea started or by who, but I can assure you with one-hundred percent confidence that no hiring manger or HR recruiter thinks this is a great idea.

Some additional tips on resumes and cover letters:

- Use the same font, heading and formatting on both the resume and cover letter.
- Make every conceivable effort to address your resume and cover letter to the correct person. You can find this out by networking, researching and calling. I understand that this might be difficult in larger corporations where the hiring manager is in a different location.

- Using keywords is not as big a deal to a hiring manager as it is to resume scanning systems. While a scanning system is programmed to search for keywords, a hiring manager will read the content of your resume. Pick out some key words and phrases from the job posting and incorporate them into your resume. (PS. Everyone is wise to the trick of copying all of the keywords and pasting them on your resume in size one font and white text. Don't do it.)
- Spell check and grammar check your documents extensively. After that, send your resume to several trusted sources and have them review and edit it.

Chapter Sixteen

Understanding Job Postings and Applying

"Choose a job you love, and you will never have to work a day in your life."
--Confucius

The best way to get your resume in front of a hiring manager is to have someone personally hand it to her or forward it with an introduction. But not everyone has this opportunity and sometimes it doesn't always work. And sometimes, people just can't find a way to network into a company.

If you must send in a resume or apply online, then that is what you will have to do. You either email in a copy of your resume and cover letter, or you go to a website and follow the instructions for applying. In either case, you are most likely going through an electronic filter of some sort that is going to scan your resume and either reject you or put you into a pile of other possible candidates.

No matter what way you are getting your resume into the company, the number one thing you can do to maximize your success is by applying only to the right jobs. I don't mean the jobs that you think are great jobs; I'm talking about the jobs that you have the necessary skills and qualifications for.

Understand that what you think you are qualified for and what the hiring company thinks you are qualified for are most likely not the same thing. We all think we can do anything, and some of us probably can, with a little time and some training. But the reality of today's job market does not always afford us those luxuries.

If you are applying for a job via some other means than someone referring you to the hiring manager, you need to go through the application process which means you must meet the qualifications listed on the job posting. The hiring manager is the only one who can bypass the qualifications, which is why you need to get it to them through some other means.

Besides the qualifications, you must also make sure this is a job you really want, because if it is not, it will become readily noticeable.

One of the big things I coach my clients on is making sure that this is a job you are indeed qualified for. And the qualifications are right there in the job posting, but some people ignore those and sell themselves on other skills. Once again, the hiring manager is the only one who can overlook any of the qualifications.

Now I will admit, there are some bad job postings out there. I've seen them go from one extreme of very limited information, to the other extreme of way too much information. So let's get right into understanding the job posting.

Who writes the job posting?

Typically, the job posting is written by the hiring manager with input from HR. The manager may pull this information from an old posting or may come up with a totally new one, depending on if this is an existing position or a brand new one. Even if this position exists already, the posting may be altered to reflect new requirements for the job.

After the hiring manager finishes their work, HR will usually take it from there and clean it up or add some requirements based on what is a general company requirement. Then they will post it online somewhere.

A typical job opening posted on a company's website is usually going to follow this simple format:

1. Introduction to the company – This is usually a paragraph or two explaining what the company does, what their products/services are, and about their culture. Not enough to get you really excited, but that is what their website is for.

2. Responsibilities of the position – This section usually spells out in some detail what you will be do doing in this position which may not be all-inclusive, but will explain what will be expected of you and what you will be evaluated on. Now just to bring out a point, because I have been asked this before, these are typically not negotiable items. Meaning, you cannot go in to the job interview and ask if some of these responsibilities can be waved. These are the duties the hiring manager is expecting you to perform. If you are not totally comfortable with doing all of these duties, then don't apply for the position.

3. Requirements/qualifications necessary for this position – This is the one section where there is some flexibility. And again, typically it is the hiring manager who has the final say on what requirements can be waived or altered. The key here is to understand the wording to see if you should even apply. The best way to do this is to look at some sample job postings and analyze them.

These are taken from actual job postings I found on the Internet - with some alterations to protect the identity of the company posting them:

- Candidate applying for the position must have Bachelor's Degree.
- Candidate must have at least 5 years of prior people management experience in a technology service
- Must have at least 4+ years with service management.
- Must have experience with medical device industry preferably imaging equipment.

The key in these 4 requirements are the words MUST HAVE. These two words indicate that the company is looking for someone with these exact qualifications. Not almost, not something like these, but these exact requirements. Not showing that you have these exact qualifications on your resume will get you kicked out faster than a Nolan Ryan fastball.

Here's another example:

- Experience in the steel industry required. Experience in stainless steel and related alloys is a plus

Again, the key word here is REQUIRED. Meaning if you have no experience in the steel industry, don't bother sending in a resume. The second sentence lists some additional experience that would be a PLUS if you have it, but is not a requirement. This means if you have this experience, your resume has moved up one more notch.

- Bachelor's degree required with preference for Instructional Design, Training and Development, or related field
- Experience in a customer service/call center environment required

The points above again have that REQUIRED label, but this time they added the word PREFERENCE. Meaning that a bachelor's degree is required (any degree) but preference will be given to those with Instructional Design.

- Demonstrated track record of positive growth in revenue, operating income and/or performance metrics preferred.

In this requirement the posting calls out that the company would prefer a candidate with this experience. However, the word DEMONSTRATED indicates that they want proof. And the proof should be something more than you copying the words and putting them in your resume. Bring some statistics with you or have a reference who can verify your record.

Qualifications: To perform this job successfully, an individual must be able to perform each essential duty satisfactorily. The requirements listed below are representative of the knowledge, skill, and ability required:

- ARR per IM
- Contribution Margin per IM
- MRR per project and at a team level

Here's a good example of requirements in a job posting that spell out some very specific qualifications. The key here is; that if you have to ask what they are, then you are not qualified for this position. The same would be true for any other kind of technical or professional position where the job posting has specific industry jargon. If you don't know what it is, then don't apply.

- Willingness to work non-traditional hours & travel (nights, weekends, holidays) with event schedule
- Ability to travel
- Ability to work remotely

These three requirements indicate that they are going to be part of your job either daily or some percentage of the time. How much time will probably be spelled out in the interview, but again, if you are not willing to do these tasks, then don't apply.

The following list are some very subjective requirements you will find in most job postings:

- Strong Organizational Skills
- Good Problem Solving Skills
- Expert at Multi-tasking
- Detail Oriented
- Strong project management experience and technical skills
- Excellent written and verbal communication skills
- Manage priorities in a constantly changing environment
- Efficient organization skills
- Expertise using MS Office applications
- Dependable, hardworking, high energy
- Effective interpersonal skills.
- Ability to work independently with a minimum of supervision

As these do not have the words required, must have, necessary, etc. anywhere in the bullet point, these are not exact requirements for a position. These are what I like to call "nice to haves". Meaning it would be great if we could find someone with all these qualifications.

Many job postings have what seems like an endless number of these types of qualifications. Don't fret if you don't have every single one of the skills required. Of course the more you have of these qualifications, the higher you will place in the maybe pile.

The hard part with these types of qualifications is understanding exactly what they mean. Words like, ability, dependable, efficient, excellent, and strong can mean different things to different people. As long as you can demonstrate that you have these skills in some way then go ahead and apply.

So here's the key to all of this. If you are emailing your resume or applying online through the company's website or through a job board, if you DO NOT have every single one of the REQUIRED qualifications, don't even send in a resume or apply. You will be saving yourself and the company a lot of time and aggravation, because you will be disqualified immediately.

However, if you have someone on the inside, someone that the hiring manager trusts, hand your resume to the hiring manager with an explanation of why you would be a great candidate despite not having all of the qualifications, then you will be ahead of the game and all of the other candidates.

Step Three – Getting the Job

"If you don't go after what you want, you'll never get it. If you don't ask, the answer is always no. If you don't step forward, you're always in the same place."
--Nora Roberts

Chapter Seventeen

Interviewing

"Big jobs usually go to the men who prove their ability to outgrow small ones."
--Ralph Waldo Emerson

This is by far *the* most important part of any job search. Everything you have done so far has gotten you to this point. Fail this, and you will be starting the process all over again. This is the point where you either get the job or you don't. It all comes down to this step.

As I've said before, there is a vast warehouse of information on this subject. But I am going to give you my opinion on the subject, from the viewpoint of a hiring manager, former job seeker and a career coach.

No matter how you got to this point, whether you sent in a resume, filled out an online application, or had someone refer you to the hiring manager, all that no longer matters from this point forward. The only thing that matters from this point forward is to prove to the employer that you are *the right person for this job.* I will repeat this point because it is the most crucial point of this whole process.

You must be *the right person for the job* in the mind of the hiring manager. She must not have any doubt that you are the one. Then, and only then, will you receive a job offer. There may be another candidate waiting in the wings if you decline, but you don't want to be that candidate. You want to be the one at the front of the line.

The interview is the obvious culmination of all your activities that you have done correctly up to this point. The fact that you have been invited to an interview should tell you one big fact; someone believes you can do the job based on the evidence you have presented to this point.

The interview process is the trial that proves that you are either the right person for the job or you are not. The hiring manager, HR and whoever else will be talking to you, will be looking for evidence to support one or the other of those statements.

Keep in mind that the information you will be reading about in this section should by no means be taken as the absolute gospel on the subject. It is given to you as a basis to prepare and win the job in the best way I know how.

Just as there are many different ways to develop a resume, there are an equal number of ways to interview for a job, not only from the job applicants viewpoint, but from the interviewers standpoint as well.

The major problem that you are going to face out there is not every interviewer is skilled at interviewing. In fact, there are a lot of hiring managers, recruiters and HR personnel who are actually bad at interviewing. They believe that the interview should be used as a way to weed out people, to trip them up at every opportunity instead of doing what they should be doing which is to find the right person for the job.

But it is not always their fault. In most cases they have been put into a position of having to hire someone with little or no training on how to do it.

The most important thing to remember about interviewing is, as I mentioned in an earlier chapter, the job search process is like the sales process. So at this stage of the process, you already have an appointment with your future customer (aka the hiring manager).

As you prepare for this step of your job search, it is important to know the number one fact about business-to-business sales. That is, a business will buy your product for one of only three reasons:

1. It will make them money
2. It will save them money
3. It will solve a problem or otherwise make their life a whole lot easier

There you have it. To succeed in the interview process you have to prove you can do one of these three things for their business. Can you make them money by designing a better product or increasing sales? Can you save them money by increasing quality or purchasing better materials for less money? Can you make their life easier by doing a job faster, safer, or with little supervision?

You need to prove that you can make them money, save them money, or solve their problem better than your competitors, i.e. the other people they are interviewing.

Since in all likelihood you are not going to know who your competitors are, your job is going to be a little tougher than a salesperson selling a product. You are going to have to sell yourself harder and better than the other job candidates.

But since you are reading this book, you will know how to do that when you are finished.

I'm going to let you in on a little secret about hiring managers – they hate to make a mistake. And there is no bigger mistake than going through the interview process, selecting a candidate, hiring them, training them, and then finding out they didn't work out.

Because now they have to not only let the person go in most cases, but they have to start the hiring process all over again. And usually the first step in the process is getting another requisition opened up, which means they have to go to their boss and admit they've made a mistake.

When you purchase some big ticket item such as a car, house or boat, you usually start out feeling really good about it. You've taken your time and selected the item and made a decision. Now, you're sitting in the finance manager's office or at the house closing and you start to second guess yourself.

"Am I making the right choice?" "Is this right for me?" What happens if.....?" All of these questions and more are filtering through your head. This is known as 'buyer's remorse'.

Well the same thing is going through the hiring manager's mind. They don't want to have buyer's remorse. So you need to do everything you can to prevent buyer's remorse in the hiring process. And the way you do this is by removing any and all doubt about you as a candidate so that the only logical choice they have is to hire you.

If there is any lingering doubt about you, you are not going to be hired. They will shop around some more before they make what could be a career-limiting decision.

To prevent buyer's remorse and to get the job offer, you need to emphatically answer these three hidden questions in every hiring manager's mind:

1. Can you do the job? (skills and experience)
2. Will you do the job? (commitment)
3. Can I work with you? (personality)

These are the three most important areas you must focus on during the interview. You need to prove that you can do the job based on your skills and experience, prove that you really want to work here and will be committed to the company, and prove that they can tolerate working with you and that you will fit in well with the people already here and to be hired in the future. Easy right?

At the end of the day, your performance during the interview process should leave little doubt in the hiring manager's mind that you are the best candidate. Hiring someone is a very risky business. Anything you can do to reduce that risk is certainly a plus in your favor. If there is any thought at all in the hiring managers mind that hiring you may be a risk, you are out.

As I said before, that fact that you were invited to an interview tells you that someone got enough information from your resume or through networking to believe that you possibly have the skills to do the job. I say possibly because anyone can write anything on a resume. And some do. The proof will come out during the interview process whether you actually know what you are doing or not. It will also come out if you really want this job and if you are someone they can stand to work with.

How you got to this point in the application process is immaterial. All of that stops at the door the minute you arrive for your interview. There is only one way to get this job and that is by proving you are the right person for the position.

Now that you have received notice of an interview, you need to do two things before you get on that phone interview or walk into that office, and that is to prepare and practice. You know that old saying "Those who fail to prepare, prepare to fail?" Well never is that a truer statement than during the interview process.

Chapter Eighteen

Preparing for the Interview

"It's not the will to win that matters—everyone has that. It's the will to prepare to win that matters."
--Paul "Bear" Bryant

Hopefully before this point you have done a thorough job of researching the company. Well whether you did or didn't you still need to do more research. Find out even more about the company. Really dig into their finances, their products and their mission. Read everything you can find on their website. Look at other job listings posted on the website. Find some common themes and identify the company's personality and culture. Find out everything you can about their competitors, their industry and their business partners. An excellent resource for this information is by reading their annual report if they are a public company.

Get the person's name that you will be interviewing with. Do a Google search, search for them on LinkedIn. Find someone in the company you can talk to about them. Find out their personality, hobbies, and work history. Not only does this give you some additional information on them, it will help you to find some talking points to carry on an interactive conversation with them.

All of that is the easy part. That is what is expected of all job candidates before they walk into an interview. But you are not like other job candidates. You are **the** candidate. You are the one that is going to get that job. But in order to do that, you are going to have to be better than other candidates. You are going to do what other candidates aren't going to do. You are going to prove to the employer that you are the candidate and that you really want this job.

While doing research on the company and the people you will be interviewing with is important, it is not the only preparation you need to do. This is just the basic stuff you will need to do before each interview with each individual company.

Preparing your list of questions

While doing your research on the company and interviewers, you should be compiling a list of questions. These questions are your back-up questions for the actual interview. The reason I say these are back-up questions is that the best questions to ask during the interview are the ones that come up naturally in conversation. These are the follow-up questions to the answers given by the interviewer.

However, you should also compile a list of questions you have about the company or the position that may not come up in the interview. I am not going to go over an extensive list of questions you should consider asking. You can search the Internet and find hundreds of questions to ask during the interview. Some questions are relatively smart questions to ask and some are - not. The difference is smart questions are the ones you come up with on your own, in your own words, about things you are really interested in. The other questions are the not-so-smart ones.

The questions you ask are part of the interview process. They are used by hiring managers, recruiters and anyone else you may interview with to make a judgment on you. They tell interviewers how you think, what is important to you, your level of maturity and emotional intelligence. If I gave you a list of questions to ask those would be my questions and not yours, so do your research and compile your own.

With all that being said, here are some guidelines on questions:

Questions to avoid asking: personal questions of the interviewer, questions on salary and vacation time.

Questions to ask: performance of the company, financial stability, expectations, work environment, and company or department culture.

Questions to ask the hiring manager: What is their management style, what type of person excels in this position, how will I be evaluated, what do they like about working there, what is the department like, what does a typical day in this position look like?

You should ask questions that you couldn't get answered somewhere else. Here's an important tip, you should never ask a question that you can readily find the answer to on the company's website. That immediately raises red flags in the mind of the hiring manager, and makes them question whether or not you are really interested in this job. It is okay to ask a questions to get more detailed information about what you read or to get some clarification, but you should never ask anything that can be found by one click of a button.

Never show up to an interview without any questions, whether it is in-person, on a telephone or on live video. Always have some questions handy to ask the interviewer. That is where the list comes in handy. Have this list with you on a phone interview and bring it with you to an in-person interview. It's perfectly okay to bring it out and refer to during an interview. It shows that you thought enough about the company and the position to come prepared.

Note: It is also perfectly okay to take notes and refer to notes during an interview. You are interviewing the company as much as they are interviewing you.

Chapter Nineteen

Preparing for Interview Questions

"It is better to look ahead and prepare than to look back and regret."
--Jackie Joyner-Kersee,

While it is almost impossible to prepare for every interview question that could be asked, there are some questions you absolutely need to prepare for and should. Again, you can search the Internet and find thousands of commonly asked interview questions. It is not necessary nor advised to find every question and get an answer for them all. That will make you sound canned and not real. Besides if you try to remember answers to all of these questions, you will fail miserably if your memory should fail you during the interview.

A better way of preparing to answer interview questions is to go over the questions you find; and try to answer some of the more difficult questions. If you can come up with most answers, then you are good to go. If you find yourself struggling to develop answers for even the easiest of questions, then read on in this chapter and the next for advice on how to develop this skill.

Besides the main three questions identified earlier, (Can you do the job? Will you do the job? Can I work with you?)

there are a couple of questions that come up time and time again from my clients that they have trouble answering:

1. Tell me about yourself.

Often, this is sometimes the first question out of an interviewer's mouth. It is especially asked first by inexperienced interviewers and those who studied the *Dumbest Interview Questions Book*. The reason this is a dumb question to ask is they have your resume right in front of them. They should already have a good idea about you.

The reason this question strikes fear in the mind of the job-seeker is we don't know how to answer it. We start asking ourselves "What is she looking for?" And usually because we don't know what they are particularly looking for, we start talking about everything, starting from our earliest childhood memories, to our current employment to our weird Uncle Ralph's antics at the last family gathering.

So before even preparing an answer to this question, you need to know specifically what they want to know. And the best way to get that information is to ask them, "What exactly do you want to know?"

You want to try to get them to be specific on what is it they want to know so you can answer the question. You don't want to give an answer that is not what they are looking for. Most of the time, they are looking for a little bit more in-depth information on your past employment. But again, if they have your resume then they should be able to ask a specific question.

Now you can keep going along this path to try and get the questions narrowed down. But what if you're unsuccessful? I had one hiring manager just ask the same question again. After that experience is when I came up with a perfect solution, I tell them a little bit about myself in a story.

Some candidates will start in with "Well I'm a hard driving, task focused, goal orientated, accountant with over 25 years of experience crunching numbers to make the books look good so that you can avoid IRS scrutiny. I'm experienced in Quick Books, Quicker Books and Fastest Books, have a BS., MBA., and a PhD.

While the above statement is accurate, it also looks like the same answer the other 10 candidates gave. So there is nothing that points to you as a *unique* individual. Certainly nothing that makes me want to take notice and hire you.

So to answer this question in a way that is unique to yourself, tell them a little story about you. One that is unique to you. One that makes you special that no other candidate is going to do.

Here's an example of an opening story I developed for myself to answer the "Tell me about yourself" question:

"From my first job bagging groceries, to being a field engineer, to managing a service organization and finally running my own business, I have been providing services to my customers. Nothing makes me feel better at the end of the day than knowing that I was able to make someone's day a little better by resolving their issue with empathy and a little bit of humor. Through the years, I have experienced many difficult situations and acquired many stories on how I

resolved these issues. I would love to share some of these with you."

In this little story, I give a little bit about my background, a little bit about what drives me as an individual, and a little bit about my personality. Also because of the way this is worded, it a great conversation starter and leaves an opening for the hiring manager to start asking some follow-up questions.

Develop your own conversation starter to answer this question. Read the section about storytelling later in this book to get more information on just how to do this.

2. What are your greatest weaknesses?

By far without a doubt, this is the dumbest question ever asked in an interview. The only reason I can see for its existence is to trip you up. Still, many inexperienced interviewers continue to ask this question so you should be prepared to answer it the correct way.

While there are several ways to answer this question, here is the one thing you don't want to do. You don't, under any circumstances whatsoever, want to go on the Internet and research answers to this question. That's even dumber than the question itself. There are two reasons for this:

The answers you are going to find are not your answers. They are canned answers. And if you use those answers, you will fail the interview.

Hiring managers use the Internet too. And you can bet that they've been on the Internet to find answers to that question. And if they hear you give one of those answers, it's not going to look favorably on you. Because they've heard all those canned answers before:

"I prefer to work on a team." *Really? Even if you can't stand the people?*

"I'm a perfectionist." *So Mr. Perfection here couldn't find a better answer than that?*

"I'm a workaholic." *Is that like an alcoholic? Am I going to have to worry about you going postal on me?*

"My greatest weakness is I tend to get too wrapped up in projects." *Well, it's a good thing that there are no projects associated with this job. But I wonder why you brought this up?*

That last one is suggested several times on the Internet by so-called "Career Experts". Their advice is to answer with something unrelated to the job, which kind of suggests that hiring managers are too stupid to figure this out. "Throw them off track by bringing up something unrelated to the job".

There really is only one way to answer this question and that is to answer it truthfully. What? Admit a fault? In an interview? You bet.

As a hiring manager, I've already identified your weaknesses. I've identified them just from reading your resume. And if it wasn't there, I've certainly identified it somewhere in our interview. So I know what your greatest weakness is as it pertains to this job. I can tell by the way you listed or didn't list a skill for this job. I can tell by the way you answered a question, by the way you had to think of an answer, or the way you avoided eye contact while talking about a skill or accomplishment. I can tell by the number of years of experience you have doing the actual work I am looking for.

What I want to know is if *you* know what your greatest weakness is at it pertains to this job. The key phrase here is *"as it pertains to this job"*. I don't really care what your weakness is outside of this. I don't care if you like housecleaning in the nude or if you like chasing greased pigs on the weekend or if your greatest weakness is chocolate ice cream. I don't care about any of that.

So if you really want to impress me, identify what your greatest weakness is for this job. Is it knowledge about spreadsheets, project management, spelling, working with customers? Whatever it is, bring it up and tell me how you are going to resolve it.

Are you going to take a class? Ask others? Read as much as you can on the subject? Tell me how you go about resolving a weakness you have. That's it. The truth is always the simplest and best answer and it is a way to continue the conversation on the subject.

A great leader is one who not only knows what they are good at but also what they are not good at, and finds a solution to that problem. Nobody can know everything and be good at everything. Hiring managers know and understand that. Here is how I would answer that question:

"As I was going over the job description, I would say that my greatest weakness would have to be working in Excel. If

120

that is a major part of my job duties, than I will find and enroll in a class and complete it within 60 days of being hired."

This is pretty straight forward. I've identified a weakness, as no doubt so has the hiring manager, I've made her aware that I am aware of this weakness, and I've offered a solution to the issue.

The great thing about this process is it will change for each job you are interviewing for. There is no need to memorize a canned response.

Note: Please do not take this answer and repeat it in an interview. This is my response. I've given you enough information to formulate your own.

3. Why did you leave your last position?

This is another tough one to answer for some people, especially if the circumstance of your leaving was not a good one.

It's easy to answer the question if you left because of a layoff or you are seeking a better career path. It gets a lot tougher if you've been fired. I've had a lot of job seekers ask me advice on this one.

And there is no easy answer. You can't hide the fact that you were fired. Oh, you probably could for a little while but eventually it will be found out. So it is best to just get it out in the open.

The best way to answer this question is to just tell the truth, just like in the other questions. I understand that in most states you can be fired for no reason whatsoever, just like you can leave a company for no reason. But companies usually don't just fire someone for no reason. There usually is a reason. Whether it is a good reason or not can probably be debated, but usually there is a reason.

So before you head into the interview, you need to be absolutely sure that you know the reason. Whatever your last company gave you as a reason is the reason. It is not what you think, or what you heard from someone else. Whatever your company told you it is the actual reason.

Once you have internalized that reason, you can start to formulate how you are going to answer it. As a hiring manager, these are the three critical things I need to hear from you on why you were let go:

1. What were the circumstances? I want to know exactly the facts as you know them. What was the reason you were let go. Don't politicize it, don't whitewash it, and don't dance around it. Tell me the background, what happened and what the results were.

2. What did you learn from this? I want to know that you understand the situation and more importantly your role in it. I want to know what you have learned from this and how you can apply that knowledge moving forward. Even if your role was miniscule, I want to know the lesson you learned even if it was to watch your back.

3. What steps have you taken to ensure this does not happen again? I want total assurance that I won't have this same problem with you. Whatever it is, you need to convince me that there is absolutely no risk of having this issue come up again.

At this point you should be quiet and let the answer linger there so that I can digest it. You can only hurt yourself by trying to add to whatever you just said. Let the silence linger and let me make the next move.

Now at this point I have two options as a hiring manager. I can accept your response and move on or ask more follow up questions about the incident until I'm ready to move on.

Most hiring managers will get to point A quickly if you've done a great job with your answer. Even if you did a really great job, there will be some interviewers who will get stuck on this and will continue to ask question after question.

Your job in all of this is to get the interviewer back on track of interviewing for this job.

After they have asked the first follow-up question and you answered it, ask them a pertinent question about the job or the company. This gives them an opportunity to answer it and hopefully get back on track. If they ask another follow-up question, answer it and immediately ask them another question to get the interview back on track.

If they persist and continue to beleaguer this point, you are running out of options. Maybe your response was not detailed enough, or the interviewer just can't get past it. At this point you need to roll the dice and ask them point blank if there was something they did not understand and if not, can we move forward with the interview.

There is no one best way to handle this situation because every interviewer is different and every situation is different. I would strongly suggest that you hire a good career coach who can help you work through this and advise you on the best way to handle your particular situation.

4. Salary questions

Let's face it, those other questions pale in comparison to this question. Every job seeker hates this question. This is another dumb question whose only purpose is to eliminate candidates. There is no other reason for it being in the interview process. Well, if you talk to enough ill-informed hiring managers and HR recruiters, you will get an answer something like this: "Well, we need to make sure that the candidate can fit into our salary range."

Really? Well if that was such an important issue to you, why didn't you post the salary range in the job description? Don't you think that applicants are smart enough to know if a salary range is acceptable to them? Or is it that you are trying to get away with finding the cheapest candidate you can? It is important that you understand the one and only purpose of this question being brought up in an interview.

There is a much better and highly intelligent way for this to be brought up in the interview process. The hiring manager or HR person should announce the salary range to the candidate. A very simple statement such as "The salary range for this position is between $60,000 to $75,000 annual. Is that a range that is acceptable to you?"

See. No hassle. It doesn't knock anyone out of the ballpark.

But let me give you the background on this little game that some companies like to play. Understand that every hiring manager knows what the salary range is for the position they are hiring for. **Every hiring manager** and every corporate HR recruiter. Those who say they don't are out-and-out lying to you. Do what you will with that information.

So why do they ask you what your salary expectations are? Because they want to get you as cheaply as they can. If their range is $60 - $75k, and you respond with $50,000, then Bingo! They've just saved $15,000 on your salary.

There is an old saying going around in the world of job search experts. "The first one to mention salary loses." I could not disagree more. Everyone loses in this scenario. There are no winners. Yet, companies continue to play this little-kids game.

I've never asked this question to a job candidate. I find it rude and disrespectful and I know it is very uneasy for the candidate. So I always throw out the salary range to the candidate and ask for verification that this range is acceptable. Of course, all things are negotiable but not during the interview. That is left for the actual job offer.

But I have had the question of "what are my salary expectations" thrown at me in plenty of interviews. So let me show you a couple of ways to handle it:

A. Interviewer: "So tell me what your salary expectations are for this position?"
Me: "I don't know. What is the salary range for this position?"

B. Interviewer: "So tell me what your salary expectations are for this position?"
Me: "I really don't know. I don't know enough about this position and the company to formulate an opinion."

C. Interviewer: "So tell me what your salary expectations are for this position?"

Me: "Well, industry standards for this position are in the range of $50,000 to $80,000. Is this your range for this position?"

Option C is a good one to use if you are uncomfortable with pushing back on the interviewer. It answers the question without being specific, and gives them a range without locking you into a specific salary. You should have a general idea what the industry standard is for this position. There are a number of ways to get salary information either by research on the Internet or through networking.

There are a couple of keys to using this option effectively:
1. Make sure that the low number is just a little below what the average is, and that the high end is larger than the average, but make sure the range is acceptable to you.
2. Make sure the range is large. At least $30,000 between the high end and the low end.
3. Make sure that the range you are indicating is indeed a range customary for your position.
4. Always make sure to ask the question at the end if this is within their range for this position.

Now that they know that you know they know, it remains to be seen what they will do about it.

Other Questions

You need to prepare for just about any other questions that may come your way. They are endless. But here is what you need to be prepared to answer:

You need to be prepared to demonstrate your proficiency (or address any weakness) on any of the qualifications listed on the job posting. Remember, you are selling yourself to a list of wants that the hiring manager is looking for. Sell yourself on the skills that are your strengths but be prepared to answer how you will resolve any weaknesses.

Be prepared to show proficiency on all the skills, accomplishments, all past positions and education listed on your resume. Anything that is on your resume you should be prepared to answer in depth. It's a little too late at this point to take something off so you need to have a good solid answer to any question that may come up.

Chapter Twenty

The Hidden Interview Questions

"We must not allow other people's limited perceptions to define us."
--Virginia Satir

Preconceived perceptions

This is an important part of the interview that not too many people are going to tell you about. But it is important that you prepare for these, because they will come up in every interview. They will come up mostly during in-person interviews, but sometimes in phone interviews.

What are preconceived perceptions?

Preconceived perceptions are those perceptions we form about other people without knowing anything about them and are based on non-factual beliefs. These are more commonly known as prejudices or biases.

Nobody likes to talk about prejudices but they are a reality for some, especially in the interviewing process. And while most people will deny it, there is always a little prejudice in all of us. Whether it is race, religion, body size, hair color, or sense of fashion, there is going to be a prejudice somewhere about it. The problem is you don't know where or when this prejudice will come up. So you had better be prepared to handle it because it is a weakness perceived by the interviewer that you will have to overcome during the interview. And every good salesperson knows what the weakness is in their product, and they know how to work around it, combat it, or make it a non-issue.

For example:

Common misperceptions about people who are overweight are:

- They are lazy.
- They have no self-control
- They can't take care of themselves.
- They have or will have health problems resulting in sick days.
- They will raise group insurance premiums.
- They have no self-respect.

Common misperceptions about older workers:

- They are behind the times.
- They are not up to speed on new technology.
- They are slow.
- They are stuck in the old ways and not open to change.
- They might retire soon.
- They have health issues.

Common misperceptions about younger workers:

- They will spend all their time on social media.
- They are party animals and will stay out late and be late for work or call in sick.
- They don't know what they are doing.
- I'm going to have to hold their hand a lot.
- They are lazy and feel they're entitled.

I think you get the idea. Now, hopefully no interviewer will raise any of these during the interview. But you can bet your first year's salary that interviewers are thinking about them. It is almost better if we could just raise these issues during the interview without the fear of being sued.

Well we can't but we are looking for evidence that these perceptions about you are not true. And the evidence has to come from you sometime during the interview. If you don't, you will not make the cut.

Remember, this is a sales process. And just like during the sales process, the buyer is going to have some objections. Some they will raise, some they won't. In a job interview, it is even tougher because in most cases, the interviewer cannot raise those objections.

A great salesperson knows everything about their product. They know the good points and the bad points. They know the competition and how the two products stack up against each other. They know what objections the customer is going to raise and they have an answer ready to combat that objection. They are prepared and ready to showcase the value of their product to the customer so that any objections they may have are overridden by the value.

On the positive side, no one knows you better than yourself. Well at least you should if you are truly honest with yourself. So as part of this process of preparing for an interview, you need to take several steps back and take a good look at yourself. Now look at yourself from the other side. What do other people see? What possible ill-conceived perceptions can they have about you? Be honest, this is no time to be an egotist.

I will use myself as an example. I am older, losing my hair and overweight. That's three strikes already against me and I haven't even walked through the door yet. But since I can see that about myself, I can figure out what the immediate perceptions are going to be; I am behind the times, lazy, and probably stuck in my way of doing things.

In fact none of these are true. But the interviewer does not know that. These perceptions are totally real, especially if the interviewer is younger, in-shape and with a full head of hair.

So I have to come to the interview prepared with enough examples of what I do and who I really am to try and offset these objections. I need to demonstrate how technically up-to-date I am by talking about all the technology I use and how up-to-date I am about the Internet and social media. I need to show how I can adapt to circumstances, new technologies and other ways of doing things. I need to prove that I'm not lazy by explaining about all the outside activities I am involved with and projects that I do to show that I don't just sit around every night watching T.V. and eating cheese puffs.

Even if you have a perfect body, your clothes are fashionable and you have all your hair, you may think you have nothing to worry about. Well think again. What if you, Mr. or Ms. Perfect, come in for an interview and the hiring manager is someone like me? Think we don't have some preconceived perceptions of you? Well guess again, we do. Everyone does to a certain extent.

This concept of preconceived perceptions is an extremely critical point that most job seekers are not aware of or think about. That is why you will fare better than the rest of them.

Now some people may have a tough time thinking about themselves in a critical way. So I am going to suggest this exercise to you. Find someone you trust who would be brutally honest with you. Find a friend, family member, co-worker or coach. Have them play the part of the hiring manager and tell you what immediate perceptions they come up with about you. Don't get hurt feelings, this is just an exercise.

Then armed with this information, start gathering all of the ammunition you are going to need to head off these objections. Being prepared for the un-raised objections is the mark of a great salesperson, the one who always gets the sale.

Realize that these objections may never get raised but they may exist in the mind of the interviewer. Your best plan to head off any of these objections is to bring so much evidence of the value you bring to the organization, that the hiring manager has no other thoughts but to hire you.

Chapter Twenty-one

Stories

"Words are how we think; stories are how we link."
--Christina Baldwin

Hiring managers love a good story. They're looking for good stories that peak their interest, invite discussion and give them an insight into the type of person you are.

In fact, a story is one-hundred times better than an explanation of your skills or achievements. A story puts things into perspective. But they don't want fiction they want facts.

Like any good story, your stories should have a beginning, a middle and an ending. In the scenario of a job search, your story should look like this:

- What was the situation? (The beginning)
- What actions did you take? (The middle)
- What was the result? (The ending)

This is commonly known as S-A-R. (Situation, Action, Result)

Like any good storyteller, your stories should capture the hiring manager's attention and keep them riveted, engaged and asking for more. Here is an example of a story following these guidelines:

"My sales numbers were down by 15% for the second month in a row. Looking at the forecast, it seemed like I was heading for a third straight month of dismal figures. Not knowing exactly what the issue was, I enlisted the help of another salesperson to go along with me on a couple of sales calls. She identified a couple of things I could do differently in my presentation. I adapted those changes and began to see my numbers come back up to where I was meeting and then exceeding my quota."

Do you see how this story flows? It identifies the situation, what actions were taken and what the results were. That covers the basics. Read that story again, but this time read it out loud to yourself. Really pay attention to what your thoughts are when hearing it. Now, write down as many questions as you can that you would want to ask the person telling you this story.

That's the beauty of a story like this, it gives just enough information to follow the SAR technique, but leaves a lot of room for follow-up questions and more lengthy conversations.

And that's the main point of a story, getting a conversation going. Conversations are much more enjoyable, comfortable and they convey more information than just answering questions. And they become invaluable, in fact they are absolutely necessary for acing behavioral interviews.

So how many stories do you need? Well you need to have at least one good story for every accomplishment you list on your resume, for every position you held, and for every item listed on the job description.

Now on this last point, it may be difficult to have a story for a requirement with which you don't have specific experience. This is why you need to have a story ready about how you overcome difficulties, how you learn new things, or what specific steps you will take to gain the knowledge necessary for this job.

The day before an interview is not the time to start developing stories about your job and your past. You must have these already put together and practiced before the interview. Besides all of the stories you will need listed in the above paragraph, you will need to have some general stories ready to go to answer the behavioral questions thrown at you.

Obviously, you cannot write and remember a story for every possible question and scenario. But you should have the major ones memorized. You don't need to memorize every word of each story exactly. The key points to memorize are the bullets of the SAR points. You can fill in the rest of the words just as you would in a normal conversation with your friends. That's why stories change over time. We remember the high points and fill in the rest as we go.

While there is a finite number of stories you can come up with, there is an infinite number of questions that can be asked in an interview. So how do you possible prepare for that?

Simple, you need to practice coming up with these on the fly. And there is no better way to practice these than with a partner. I'll cover this in more detail in the next section.

One final note on storytelling: the stories have to be real, truthful and most importantly they have to be about you. You cannot take what happened to Joe the sales guy, or Sally who manages the Accounting Department and make them yours. They have to be totally about you (and your team) and the actions you took. So start putting together your own storybook of your career.

Chapter Twenty-two

Practicing for the Interview

"When you are not practicing, remember that someone somewhere is practicing, and when you meet him he will win."
--Ed MacAuley

Practicing for an interview is absolutely the most important step you can do to win an interview. And make no mistake about it, I can spot someone who has not practiced for an interview in a few seconds. And so can most experienced well-trained interviewers.

Everyone needs to practice before an interview. Just like professional athletes, musicians, speakers; and just about anyone who wants to succeed, you need to practice, practice, and then practice some more.

But like anything, there is a right way and a wrong way to practice. The wrong way is to go over your notes while sitting in the lobby waiting for the hiring manager to come get you. The right way is to practice every possible answer and story that may come up days in advance of the interview.

Even if you are called today for an interview tomorrow, you should be well rehearsed before that interview. Practicing is not a one-and-done kind of thing. It is perpetual, meaning you should be practicing some part of your interviewing skills every day. That way, when they call you in on a moment's notice, you will be prepared and ready to go with only a few very specific points to go over.

Once you have created your stories and gone over your answers, you need to practice saying them. And I don't mean silently to yourself, I mean out loud so that you can hear yourself. It is extremely important to practice your responses out loud, it is the only way to get them through to yourself. Here's what I mean.

When you just read something, you are only using one of your senses to review the material and that is your eyesight. While it is important, it is not as important as using your sense of hearing also. When you listen to yourself speak, your brain can pick up on all the little nuances that are coming out of your mouth. It can interpret the way you are saying something, your volume, your pronunciation, your flow of words. All of these things can be registered by your brain which should in turn, alert you to any obscurities.

But sometimes, that is not enough. Sometimes you need more input. So get an audio recorder or even better, a video recorder. Record yourself answering questions and telling your stories. Play the tapes back and listen for how your voice flows. Do you pause too often, stumble on your words, do you not sound confident? Study each of these qualities and make adjustments.

Scaling it up one step, have a partner help you with this. Have them role play the part of an interviewer while you are being recorded, then watch or listen to the playback together. Make sure your partner notes all of the mistakes you make or ways you can sound better.

Scaling it up even more, go through a mock interview with a professional coach. They will record the interview and offer suggestions and guidance on what to change and how to best present yourself.

Sounds like a lot of work doesn't it? Well yes, yes it is. But if you want that job, you need to put in the effort. And believe me, your effort in preparing yourself and practicing will shine through in the interview.

Chapter Twenty-three

Acing the Interview

"You have to have confidence in your ability, and then be tough enough to follow through."
--Rosalynn Carter

Now that you have spent all this time preparing and practicing for an interview it is time for the real thing. This is the moment you've been waiting for; an opportunity to talk to the hiring manager. All of your hard work researching and preparing has gotten you to this point. Now all you have to do is get through the interview without messing up.

Let me ease your mind a bit by telling you that almost nobody gets through an interview without making a mistake or saying the wrong thing. I know I've made mistakes during interviews and most hiring managers will probably admit to making a few themselves. The key is to limit the number of small miscues you make while avoiding any major ones.

Most well trained experienced hiring managers, whose main goal is to find the right person, will overlook an assortment of miscues during an interview. Unfortunately, I cannot tell you which mistakes those are because they will differ from individual to individual. What I think is an acceptable blunder might be an unacceptable one to another hiring manager.

My main point I want to get across to you is this: relax. Don't get yourself all flustered thinking that you have to get everything right in an interview. Your main focus should always be on your content. Well thought out responses and stories along with strong communication skills will usually win over the minds of hiring managers. That's not to say what you wear or how you sit is not important, they are, but hopefully your content will overcome any mistakes in this area.

There is an infinite amount of material available on the Internet, in your local library and in book stores that will teach you all about what to wear, how to act, how to sit, what makeup you should have and what to bring. My goal in this book is not to teach you all of those things the other books do. My goal is to show you how to impress the hiring manager to get her to hire you.

So let me net out the whole "what to do during an interview" into something more manageable. Here are the important things:

1. *Be respectful and courteous to everyone you meet*
2. Dress appropriately for the position in clean well-fitting clothes
3. Arrive five minutes early
4. Bring all of your supporting material to the interview
5. Follow-up with thank you notes and/or emails
6. *Relax*

Being respectful is hugely important because you never know who is in on the interview process. The person you bump into on the elevator might be one of the people interviewing you. The receptionist might be part of the process. While they might not actually sit in on the interview, there is a really high chance that someone will ask them what they observed of you while you were waiting. I personally know several hiring managers who will ask the receptionist, the security guard, the shuttle driver and anyone else the candidate came in contact with on how that candidate treated them. Consequently, several good candidates were taken out of consideration for the position because they treated someone rudely.

And relaxing is even more important. When you are stressed out, your brain tends to not think straight. That is when all of the bad stuff happens which then just builds up more stress which causes more bad stuff to happen.

So learn some relaxation techniques. Some that I found to be helpful are deep breathing, taking a leisurely walk outside around the building; (not a power walk, a slow paced one), standing while waiting for the interview; and humming a relaxing song to myself. In short, find what relaxes you and do it before the interview.

Now remember, you are in this interview because someone saw enough evidence in your resume that you have the skills necessary to do this job. The purpose of the interview is to find out if you are the right person for this job.

So to refresh your memory, there are three main questions you must answer during the interview:

1. Can you do the job? (skills and experience)
2. Will you do the job? (commitment)
3. Can you work with us? (personality)

All of your preparation work of developing answers to questions, stories and questions to ask will take of the first two questions. That leaves you with getting past the third one. This is taken care of by what I call the three C's.

Character – What are you like as a person? Are you a team player? Can you fit into our culture? What are your values?

I will find out all about your character through our conversation and by doing a background check on you. But the most important one is the feel I get for you during the interview. How you respond to questions, what responses you give, how you handle yourself all come into play. And yes, they are all subjective. That is why you need to come armed to the interview with your most important weapon: yourself.

Bring your personality, your charisma, your background, your experiences and your humor. In other words bring yourself. Don't bring someone you are not. If you fake it during the interview and pretend to be someone you're not, it will come out during the first week on the job. And if you're not a fit, if you turn out to be someone other than the person I interviewed, then it will turn out badly for both of us.

Commitment - What is your level of commitment to this job? To the company? To their mission statement and their vision?

In other words are you totally on-board with everything the company does and stands for? This includes their products, their processes, their customers and their people.

You should have done enough research and talked to enough people prior to the interview to answer these questions. So hopefully you are okay with everything about the company and can show that during the interview. At this point, the hiring manager is looking for evidence that you are committed to this company and are not going to be job shopping your first week there.

Confidence – Can you do the job? And any other job I throw your way? Can you find your own way around or will I have to hold your hand the whole time you are here?

Confidence is one of the most important tools you can bring to a job interview. If you don't have confidence in yourself, how can I as the hiring manager, have any confidence that you are the right person for this job? I need to be absolutely sure that you can handle this job; and any other job that may come up in the future.

Now just as a point of clarification, there is a huge difference between confidence; and arrogance. Don't tell me that you can handle any job I throw your way, that you've never found a situation you couldn't handle or that you have no weaknesses. This is arrogance. I don't hire arrogance I hire confidence.

So what is confidence? And more importantly, how do you get it?

Confidence is the belief in one's powers or abilities, either believing in your own or someone else's abilities. In the interviewing process, you need to communicate to me that you are confident, and I need to be confident in you.

Confidence in oneself is not something where you can flip a switch and instantly have. It is something that is built up over a period of time. And you are the only one who can build your self-confidence. Again there is an abundance of information on how to build self-confidence and it is too lengthy of a subject to get into in a few short paragraphs here. But if you are really stuck on this and have low confidence in yourself, then I would suggest you contact me. I am trained to help individuals improve their self-confidence.

But let me give you one quick tip on improving your self-confidence; stop thinking negative thoughts about yourself! And anything else!

This is the biggest detriment I see when working with clients. The negative thoughts come through in an instant. I can see it in their eyes, in their posture and in their speech. I can tell by their actions if you they confident or not. Most of these can be overcome and your confidence will dramatically improve by thinking positive thoughts.

There are two ways to communicate confidence that come into play during an interview - physical and verbal.

Let's start with the physical. This is easy. It is the way you dress, the way you stand, the way you walk and the way you sit. It's natural to be a little stressed during an interview. An unconfident person will be tensed and uncomfortable. A confident person will make themselves comfortable, but still formal, so that they can be relaxed and at their very best.

It starts when you are entering the building. Are you walking upright confidently, or are you slouched over walking slowly? Are you walking with a purpose or are you walking like you're trying to avoid something?

How are you standing? Are you erect, hands clasped in front of you, feet slightly apart? Or are you again slouching, hands rigidly at your side, or in your pockets?

Are you smiling? Or do you look like you would rather be anyplace but here?

When you sit, are you sitting as rigid as a statue in a park, or are you relaxed and ready to go? Are your hands placed comfortably on your side, the arm of the chair or on top of the conference table?

Verbally communicating confidence is perhaps the greatest thing you can do in a job interview. Being confident with verbal communication can be the one that most people struggle with. I'm not talking about answering the questions about your background or how you saved the company boatloads of money. I'm talking about the "selling the sizzle" part. This is the part that is going to convince a hiring manager that you are the right person for the job.

There are several things that communicate self-confidence to a hiring manager during a job interview:

Doing what is right even if you are ridiculed for it – Confident people stand apart from the crowd and don't settle for the status quo. Talk about a time where you didn't follow the crowd or didn't do what everyone else does because it just didn't feel right.

Taking risks and going the extra mile – Tell a story of when you went out of your way to help a customer or an associate. Give examples of times when you took a risk at work and explain the outcome even if it turned out bad.

Admitting your mistakes – Everyone knows when they make a mistake or when they don't know the answer to something. Confident people are not afraid to admit they made a mistake and will learn from these actions. Tell the hiring manager a story of a mistake you made and what you learned from it.

Giving credit where credit is due – If you played a major role in the success of a something, don't be afraid to tell about it. At the same time, if you played a minor role, make sure to note that as well and talk about the work that others did.

Above all of this, the other main thing you can do to boost your confidence is to prepare and practice.

Confidence = Prepare, Practice, and Repeat as many times as necessary.

I cannot stress the importance of preparing and practicing for an interview enough. Besides, learning about the company and coming prepared with answers to questions and questions to ask, being prepared will give you a huge confidence boost going into a job interview.

All of the information I've covered in this chapter shows you how to prove you can do the job to the hiring manager. Who in the end; is the ultimate decision maker. Certainly, there are some instances where the final decision rests with someone higher up. In that case, use these same strategies to win them over.

Other Interviewing Advice

Have a plan. Make sure you know exactly what you want to say and ask. Don't just show up to the interview and start talking uncontrollably and asking irrelevant questions just to have something to say. Make your presentation meaningful to the recipient.

Don't show up with an attitude. Yeah, your last company did you a dirty by letting you go, but this is a new company and a new beginning. Treat it as such.

Don't text or answer your phone while interviewing. In fact, leave all of your electronic devices in the car or at home. This includes cell phones, pagers, laptops, tablets and anything else that requires electricity of some kind or that makes noise. Unless you are applying for a job as a technical specialist and need to show some sample code, leave it at home. Print out whatever presentation or material you want to show me. Then you can leave it with me so I can look it over more closely later.

While the one-on-one interview is the most important part of the whole interview process, it is not the only interview you will encounter during the hiring process. While most of these aforementioned skills come into play with these other interviews, there are some new things to think about and things you will need to prepare for in order to succeed.

Chapter Twenty-four

The Phone Interview

"The success of your presentation will be judged not by the knowledge you send but by what the listener receives."
--Lilly Walters

No matter what your personal feelings are about phone interviews, they are almost a sure thing that this is the first interview you are going to have with your perspective employer. Personally I hate phone interviews. I hated them as a hiring manager and I hated them as a job seeker because they are impersonal. But still they are a necessary part of the interviewing process.

The most important tip I can give you for the phone interview is to relax. Because you cannot see the person on the other side of the phone, you cannot gauge how you are coming across, or their reaction to anything you are saying. Are they confused, angry, bored? You get no immediate visual feedback. This might cause some people to become even more nervous. So here are my tips on overcoming some of the nervousness on a phone interview.

1. Prepare yourself by having all of your information handy; resume, job posting, research. Have it spread out and available to refer to.

2. Have your answers prepared and practiced as well as your list of questions.
3. Stand up (if you can). Never do a phone interview sitting down. Sitting down contracts your stomach, lungs and vocal chords. Standing up allows your body to relax and lets you breathe deeper and easier.
4. Use a cordless phone. This allows you to move around a little which also helps to relax you. It also lets you use your hands to gesture. No one will see you, but it helps relax you and puts some emphasis on words. Better yet, a cordless headset if you have one. Note: Make sure the batteries are fully charged and your device works.
5. Make sure you are away from distractions. Lock out the kids, dogs and significant others; turn off the T.V., radio, and cell phones (yes I have done a phone interview where the applicant had a T.V. set on in the background); make sure the room is a comfortable temperature.

I've even gone to the extreme of leaving my house, finding a nice quiet place to park and doing a phone interview there. Yes, it goes against the advice of standing, but the fact that I was alone and in a quieter place was a better option at the time.

One of the keys to passing the phone interview is to know who you are interviewing with and what role they play in the interview process. In the best of situations, the person doing the phone interview will be the actual hiring manager. In this scenario you have a better idea of the questions that may be asked of you , and you can prepare the questions you would normally ask a hiring manager.

The next level down is a recruiter within the HR department of the company you are applying to. While not optimal, they at least know about the company and can answer your questions about it. And hopefully you will be able to find some information about the interviewer by doing some research on them.

The worst case scenario is if the company is using an outside third party to do the initial interview screening. I say this because they are usually working from a scripted set of questions and cannot rephrase them so that you can get a better understanding of what they are looking for. Even worse, they cannot typically answer anything but the first level questions about the company. Since they don't work for them, they don't know a lot about them. Your best shot at passing this type of interview is to just answer the questions directly.

The number one thing you need to ask before the phone interview begins is who you are interviewing with and the role they have within the organization.

Another note on phone interviews – never do a phone interview on the spur of the moment. If an interviewer calls and wants to do a phone interview right then and there, politely work with them to schedule it for another time. You don't ever want to do a phone interview when you are not fully prepared and ready. Use whatever phrasing you want to (just heading out, you have visitors, etc.) in order to reschedule the interview. Practice this answer so it sounds natural and don't back down. Most interviewers will work with you to schedule another time.

Chapter Twenty-five

Other Types of Interviews

"Eight-five percent of the reason you get a job, keep that job, and move ahead in that job has to do with your people skills and people knowledge."
--Cavett Robert

Group/Panel Interviews

These are by far the most stress-inducing interviews which is why some companies choose to do them, to see how you handle stressful situations. If you can remain calm and answer the questions you will most likely survive this round.

The key point here again is to prepare for them as much as possible. Some companies will let you know in advance that there will be a group interview. Others won't and will spring it on you when you walk in. This is not the time to think "Darn, I should have prepared for this."

Before starting the interview, ask for everyone's business card or get their name and title. You want to be able to refer to them by name during the interview. Arrange the cards or write their names in the order in which they are sitting. During the interview you will be asked questions by several people in the group. Start answering by first looking directly at the person who asked the question, but slowly attempt to look at every person in the group as you continue.

One of the favorite "games" some companies like to use is to insert a disinterested person in the group. This person might be on their phone, reading email or otherwise be doing something other than being involved in the interview. This is just a trap used to get you stressed or to fluster you. Just ignore this person until they actually ask a question, but do include them in your answer by glancing at them as you speak. Another favorite trap is the old "good interviewer/bad interviewer" scenario where someone in the group is there to trip you up and make you nervous. Be aware of these types of situations and practice for them.

To practice and prepare for these kinds of interviews, just find 3-5 friends, relatives or enemies who are willing to rake you over the coals during a practice interview round. Well you don't want them to be that rough, but you also don't want them to be nice and lob softies at you. They need to ask tough questions and rapidly fire them at you because this is the way it could be during the real thing.

If you can, have these sessions videotaped so your performance can be evaluated. Then do it again and again until you are performing as cool as a cucumber and don't get rattled. Again, you may never encounter a group interview. But it is still better to be prepared.

Behavioral Interviews

Sometimes also referred to as situational interviews, behavioral interviews are typically just questions that require you to think of certain times or events and explain what happened, what you did and what was the outcome. A lot of these questions are asked in a normal interview, but in some cases, they are the only questions that are asked.

They are designed to give the interviewer an idea of how you think, what your thought processes are; and how you react to certain situations. Again, you can do further research on behavioral interviews, but if you have followed the previous steps in this book of developing stories, acing a behavioral interview will be like a walk in the park.

Just to give you a feel for the types of questions that could be asked, here a few examples:

1. Give me a specific example of a time when you were able to persuade someone to see things your way.
2. Describe the system you use to keep yourself organized and able to complete tasks.
3. What time management process do you use to make sure you meet your deadlines?
4. Tell me about a time you disagreed with your boss.
5. Describe the most significant presentation that you have had to complete.
6. Tell me about a time when you failed to meet a deadline. What things did you fail to do and what did you learn?
7. What has been your greatest challenge?
8. Tell me about a time when you successfully resolved conflict in the workplace.

9. What makes you think you can handle this position?
10. What can you contribute to this company?
11. What are your short-term goals and how to do plan to achieve them?
12. What is your most significant accomplishment to date?
13. If I asked the people who know you best for one reason I shouldn't hire you, what would they say?
14. Describe a stressful situation at work and how you handled it.
15. How do you handle a company policy that you don't agree with?

The list is endless and you can spend several days researching them all on the Internet and in books.

There are two keys to acing the behavioral interview:

1. Have that list of stories we talked about earlier in the back of your head so you can formulate an answer.
2. Practicing how to answer these questions is the best preparation you can do to survive it.

The Lunch Interview

This is treated like any other interview, except you are having it at a place other than the office. Prepare for it the same way as you would for any other interview. But there are a few rules of etiquette to follow if you are having an interview during lunch or even dinner.

- Do not order an alcoholic beverage. Not even a non-alcoholic type beverage such as a Virgin Mary or non-alcoholic beer. Stick with soft drinks, coffee, tea or better yet water. Even if the interviewer is imbibing, don't do it.
- Do not offer to pick-up the check. It is the interviewer's responsibility to pay for the meal.
- Do not order any kind of messy food such as spaghetti with sauce or anything that requires you to hold the food in your hand. Order something that you can easily eat with a fork and not spill on yourself or the person next to you.
- Order something even if you are not hungry. If you are nervous, order a glass of water and a small salad or something. Nibble at it if you have to but don't leave the interviewer hanging as the only person eating.
- Don't talk with your mouth full of food. I know I shouldn't have to mention this at this stage of your life, but I have witnessed this personally during an interview. Besides, chewing your food thoroughly and swallowing gives you time to formulate a good answer if asked a question.
- Pace your conversation with the other person. Don't ask them a question when they just chucked a whole cheeseburger into their mouth. Wait until they have chewed and swallowed their food before continuing.

- Be courteous to everyone in the restaurant from the parking attendant to the wait staff to the busboy, even if the interviewer is not there. Again, I shouldn't have to mention it, but I feel I must. This could be the interviewer's favorite restaurant and she just might ask around about you afterwards.
- Turn off all electronic devices and do not under any circumstances answer your phone or send a text while you are at the interview. Even if the interviewer gets on their phone, wait patiently until they are done.

Skype and Video Interviews

These are becoming more popular as companies are looking at ways to cut costs and interview candidates that live outside of their local areas. Prepare for these interviews the same way you would prepare for other interviews. Because these involve technology, the key here is to make absolutely sure that your technology is working before the interview. I don't mean five minutes before the interview, I mean days before. And check it several times after that.

Another key thing to note is where you position your camera for the interview. Remember that the camera can see things behind you so make sure that the background is either a blank wall or at least something professional. A bookcase with business books or some awards or diplomas will do nicely. Have your notes ready and remember to relax.

Chapter Twenty-six

Asking for the Job and Following Up

"Sure it's a big job; but I don't know anyone who can do it better than I can."
--John F. Kennedy

Asking for the Job

The number one failure of all job seekers is also one of the easiest things you can do. That is asking the hiring manager for the job, if you want it.

Just like the salesman will never get the sale if they never ask the prospect for it, you will never get the job if you don't ask for it.

I don't mean getting down on your knees and begging for it. I mean a simple one line phrase that at least tells the interviewer that you are interested. You and I both know that there are other candidates and there are other job opportunities. If you are interested and wish to continue further along this process, just tell them.

"Mary, from everything I've seen about your company and in talking with you today, I am very interested in pursuing this process further and would be excited to work for you and Acme Turbo Forks if an agreement can be reached."

Just keep it simple and let them know that you are interested in working there if they think you are the one and you can both agree on terms.

Of course, if you are not interested at this point, then by all means feel free to let them know that too. There is no point in continuing any further if you decide this is not the right company, position, or manager for you. No hard feelings, shake hands and move on.

Remember, a hiring manager's job is to find the best person for the job. This might take a while, several months in most cases. The whole bunch of interviewees might not be the right person and they may have to start all over again. Sometimes, there is just that one little thing that makes you almost the right person, but they don't know how that pans out until they talk to everyone. So hang in there.

Following Up

This is the part that really throws some job seekers for a loop. When should I follow up? How often should I follow up? Should I just wait or initiate some contact? How much is too much? It's sometimes extremely confusing, especially when you don't hear anything.

Let's face it. There are a lot of companies that are bad at following up after interviews and some that don't do it at all. Let me just tell you where I stand on this issue.

There is no excuse for a company, recruiter or hiring manager to not follow up with their interviewees. It is disrespectful and just bad business and in the end they will make a reputation for themselves. In the meantime, there are only so many things you can do to follow up and get an answer.

I remember a job interview I went on once. I had an initial phone interview and then was invited to come out to their headquarters outside of Denver, Colorado. They flew me out there and back, picked up the ground transportation, took me to lunch and set up a whole day of interviews with different people within the organization. My chief contact who was also the hiring manager was a V.P. with the company.

After all that, it was quite disturbing to not get one form of communication from the company at all. Not from the V.P., not from HR, not from any of the other people I met. It was like they had gone out of business.

After several unanswered phone calls, email and voice mails, I had basically written them off of my list. Then about two months after the interview, I happened to catch the V.P. at his desk when he picked up the phone. The basic reply was "we have still not found the right person for the job yet."

"So does this mean I am out of the running for this position?" I asked. "No we haven't eliminated anyone yet. We are bringing in a new batch of interviewees starting in a couple of weeks," came the reply.

"Well," I said, "Let me make this easier for you. I am no longer interested in working for you or your company so just take my name off of your list."

I had no idea if my name was still on his list or not. The point is that if they went to the expense of flying me out for an interview, they could at least take thirty seconds to send me an email letting me know what was going on. I did not want to work for a company that could not do something as simple as that.

So here is what you need to do as far as follow-up is concerned.

A. Try to set a date with the interviewer on when is a good time to follow-up or ask when you should expect to hear something. If no date has been set, wait at least two weeks before initiating any contact.

B. If that date has passed, send a gentle reminder email to the interviewer asking for a status update and let them know you are still interested.

C. If you don't hear back in a week or two, then send another gentle reminder.

That's all you need to do. Don't continue on with more emails, phone calls or visits. If you don't hear something back after the second email, then you need to reconsider whether you want to work for this company. This might be an indication of what you could expect once you are an employee.

Until you receive a written job offer from the company you do not have a job there. It is imperative that you continue on with your current job, which is to find a job.

Chapter Twenty-seven

Communication Skills

"The greatest problem in communication is the illusion that it has been accomplished."
--George Bernard Shaw

Throughout the entire job search process you are going to be constantly communicating with someone in some form or another. This communication is going to have a dramatic impact on your success in landing a new job. Whether that impact is going to be positive or negative depends entirely on how effective and skilled you are in your verbal and written communications. All of your hard work to this point could be negated if you fail to communicate effectively.

Every single hiring manager and recruiter I have ever talked to points to communications as the single most important aspect of the hiring process that will either move a candidate forward or eliminate them. The words you speak and write tell a lot about you as a candidate. They leave a vivid and lasting impression of your confidence, your intelligence, your maturity and your professionalism.

The ability to communicate correctly is by the far the most important skill you can use to impress a hiring manager. That's why I felt it was vitally important to point this out to you and give you a chance to correct it before you embarrass yourself in an interview and wind up losing a great opportunity.

How can you impress upon the hiring manager that you are the right person for the job if you cannot effectively and confidently communicate that to them? You may have the best words put together to answer their questions, but if you don't confidently verbalize them, what good are they?

One of the biggest errors that reflects a lack of confidence when speaking is to use what is known as filler words. These are the *um's, ah's,* the *you knows* and the worst filler word of all, *like*. Like when people like aren't sure of what to like say next, they um, ah, like to, say like a lot. Like I just did. Did you like that? Think how annoying it is for the hiring manager to hear like five times in every sentence.

If you use the word "like" in a sentence and you are not comparing two things, or you are not explaining something that you enjoy, then I am not going to hire you because you are coming across as an airhead. And I don't want to hire an airhead. Sometimes we can't tell right away that you are an airhead, but this one is a dead give-away.

Sorry, there is no other way to put it. This is intended to hit you hard and wake you up.

Let me be perfectly blunt with you because someone needs to be. If you cannot put two sentences together without inserting the word "like" or if you cannot start a sentence without using the word "like" then I have some bad news for you. You are 'likely" not going to get the job.

If after every sentence you ask me if "you know" , then I am going to ask you if "you know" where the exit door is or do I have to walk you to it? Because when you ask me repeatedly if I know (You Know) then you are either asking me if I know something or implying that I already do. In either case you are annoying me already in this short interview and I'm certainly not going to hire you and be treated to this every day.

Stumbling over your own words and, using improper or wrong words or using them incorrectly, inserting a swear word are further examples of lack of confidence and could cost you the job. Um's and ah's are equally as deadly.

Why do these situations come up in our conversations? Two reasons: the first is we are not prepared, and the second is we engage our mouths before we engage our brains. We get to a point where our brain is finally catching up and telling our mouths to hold up a second, and when this happens, we fill in this absence of anything useful to say with the words like um, ah, like and you know.

Here is how you can correct that situation. Keep your mouth closed and think of your next words. Inserting a second or two of silence in between words is a lot better than using the word like. It shows that you are thinking of the right thing to say instead of blathering on. Take a couple of seconds before answering the questions to formulate your answer before you begin speaking. That way, you won't have to ask the interviewer if they can understand the words that are coming out of your mouth.

Using silence is a very powerful tool in conveying confidence. It says I am confident in what I am saying, and a couple of seconds of silence is not going to make me uncomfortable. By the way, this is a favorite tool of some interviewers to try and trip up the interviewee. After the question is answered they sit there in silence hoping that the applicant will continue on and blurt out something that doesn't make sense or worse, contradicts what they just said.

Silence makes some people uncomfortable and then they begin to think, "Maybe I didn't answer the question correctly" or "They must be looking for more." Don't fall for this trick. If there is an uncomfortable silence, ask them a question.

Besides being able to speak effectively, you also need to listen effectively. If done poorly this skill will result in you losing points with the hiring manager. What do I mean by listening? I mean paying attention to what the other party is saying or asking. It means waiting until they are done talking before you try to jump in with an answer. It means validating what the other person just said so that you can formulate the correct response.

If you want to get ahead in the world and get that dream job of yours, you need to be at the top of the communication ladder. I'm not saying that you have to be perfect, but you have to be better than your competition if you want to win the job race.

If you really want to improve your communication skills and take them to the next level, I have just the answer for you. Find the nearest Toastmasters club and join it today. Some people may have the wrong impression of Toastmasters so let me just clear up the confusion right now.

Yes, Toastmasters is an organization that helps you improve your public speaking skills. But public speaking is not about standing on a stage in front of a large audience and pumping them full of motivation and inspiration. That is paid speaking and it is a career not a hobby. And only about

1% of the 250,000+ members even go on to making it a career, and even less actually succeed at it.

Public speaking is the act of communicating with another human being, one-on-one communications. That is what Toastmasters helps you to improve on, the ability to speak and listen effectively.

And even more important to job seekers is how Toastmasters can teach you how to speak off-the-cuff, how to listen to a question and formulate an answer in a clear concise manner. Learning this skill is invaluable for the interviewing process. But perhaps the greatest improvement you can gain from joining Toastmasters is self-confidence. It has been my personal experience, and of many other members I have spoken to, that mastering the ability of speak in front of a group with authority, sincerity and persuasion, provides the greatest boost to your self-confidence that I have ever witnessed.

Besides speaking effectively, it is just as important to write effectively. Whether it be a resume, cover letter, an email, website or your profile on LinkedIn, every piece of written communications you send out into the world is a reflection on you. This is true not only in the job search process, but also in your everyday work.

Take the time to make sure that the words you write are spelled correctly, and that you are using the correct form of the word, (there, their, they're). Make sure you are using correct grammar and punctuation and that you are using words and phrases in the correct manner. While using spell check may catch many of these mistakes, any important correspondence you put out there should be proof-read by a knowledgeable source.

Taking this step can make all the difference in the way you are perceived by the world. That's why I had several people proof-read this book and sought out and hired a professional to edit it; to catch all my mistakes before I put it out there. Commit to honing your communication skills and improving your life

Why am I so big on communications? How else do you think you can convince a hiring manager that you are the right person for the job?

That's what it's all about.

Chapter Twenty-eight

Selling the Sizzle

"I've learned that people will forget what you said, people will forget what you did, but people will never forget how you made them feel."
--Maya Angelou

There is a phrase that I heard while learning about sales and marketing, "Sell the sizzle, not the steak."

What this means is that most people don't go to a steakhouse because they want steak, they go there for the experience of eating steak. They want that plate coming out of the kitchen and being put in front of them, with a baked potato loaded with their favorite toppings and a big old steak knife on the side.

And the steak, cooked exactly the way they like it, hot and still sizzling on the plate. Sell the sizzle not the steak.

Great salespeople understand that features are features and options are options. And if all of the competitor's features are all the same, the customer might as well just go with the least expensive product. What they sell their customer on is the benefit and experience of owning their product.

Let's face it, while your skills are definitely a big part of proving that you can do the job, hammering a nail is hammering a nail. Unless you have a way of hammering a nail that is vastly superior to everyone else, then you are just another nail hammerer.

Let's go back to our steakhouse. If you wanted to eat steak, you could just go down to the local market and buy one and cook it at home. Or you could go to one of those low budget steakhouses which are just one step above cooking it at home.

But you go to that great steakhouse not because you want to eat steak, but because you want the experience. You want to smell the steak when you first walk in. You want to open that menu and choose the cut of meat and your favorite sides. You want great service. You want the feel of cutting into it and taking that first bite, and you want someone to clean your plate off of the table when you are done.

That is what you want to sell to the hiring manager. You want to paint a great picture in her mind of what it would be like to have you as an employee. You want her to picture the fact that she can give you an assignment, that you will handle it with minimum supervision, that you will get it done right and on time, that if you make a mistake that you will own up to it and clean up the mess.

You want her to envision that you are able to handle things, that she can take her of her business because you are taking care of yours, that you are a self-starter and passionate about this job and working at her company. Most importantly, you want her to picture that you are the right person for this position.

That is selling the sizzle.

Chapter Twenty-nine

Conclusion

"It's never too late to be what you might have been"
--George Eliot

"The minute you settle for less than you deserve, you get even less than you settled for."
--Maureen Dowd

I hope I gave you enough information in the pages of this book to help you get the job you want. This book could have easily been three or four times as long. I could have written it in such a way that gave you step-by-step instructions on how to do everything in every chapter. But that would not have gotten you any further in your job search. It is impossible to cover every single situation in any book, lecture or training class on the subject of job searching.

I'm sure that you found some topics in this book easy to comprehend and some not so easy. That is because every individual is different and their situations are going to be unique to them. There is no one generic job search process nor are there generic answers to every situation.

That is why is it of the utmost importance that you engage the services of a qualified career coach to help you through this process. Yes, they cost money. But so does being unemployed. If you weigh the cost of hiring a coach versus the cost of being unemployed for months and months, I'm sure you will see that the cost will be quickly reimbursed by finding a higher paying job in less time than going it alone. A good coach will work closely with you to identify your skills, develop a marketing plan, review your resume, practice your interviewing skills and answer the questions that pertain to your unique situation.

A job search is a very stressful situation especially if you are going at it alone. I know, I tried that once before. The good news is that there are people out there who can help you through this process. Seek their help and guidance and you will be employed quicker.

There is a job out there for everyone. I truly believe that with the right focus, mindset, attitude and self-confidence, you can find the work you want to do. You have to keep an open mind and be totally honest with yourself. Maybe your perfect job is not a job at all. It might be that you are ready to take on the world by owning your own business.

Take a deep hard look inside yourself and open up that internal vision of what you want your life to be. Life is too short to settle for just any job. There are plenty of "cubicle zombies" out there. You know the ones I'm talking about. They come in through the same doors, take the same path to their desks, walk the same line to get their coffee or eat lunch, then take the same way home. Repeat for the next thirty years.

Don't get me wrong, if that is what you want, then great. Go for it, I will cheer you along every step of the way. What I want to make sure of is that you are sure that is truly what you want and not something that you just settled for because you couldn't find anything else.

"Cubicle zombies", as I refer to them, all have one thing in common, they are in their comfort zone and will never leave it. Once you enter your comfort zone and stay there, you can't expect anything to change. In order for something to change, you have to change. You have to be willing to get out of that comfort zone and try something different.

That involves risk and risk takes courage. Courage to do something no one else has. You should think, "Why not" instead of "Why I shouldn't." Everything we have today, we have because someone had enough courage to take a risk and try something different. The risk takers are the ones who will change our world, and they are the ones who will rightly benefit from taking that risk.

Finding a new job is a difficult business these days. The winners will be the ones who are willing to step out of their comfort zone and go about this business in a different way. The winners will not settle for anything less than getting what they want.

I truly believe that if you adapt and follow the principles that I have shown you in this book, you will indeed be one of the winners, and you will end up at a place that makes you come alive, if you have the courage to take control of your job search.

This is your life, live it, live big.
I wish you all success.

Tom Nosal

Resources

My coaching business, Scaling Up, provides private one-on-one and group coaching to job seeker, managers and business owners. Just like a dedicated athlete, having a personal coach during your job search will allow you to quickly achieve your goals of getting the job you desire. Together we can discover what is keeping you from having success, develop a focused plan, and continually review and adjust as necessary to get you the success you desire. For more information go to www.scalingupsuccess.com and fill out your information on the contact us page.

The following information is provided as a service to the readers of this book to further help you in your job search and career development. I receive no income or payment from these resources, however, I am very familiar with the services they provide and the work they do is phenomenal.

Soft skills are vital to finding a job, working in that job and advancing your career.

Hayward Suggs adds velocity to personal and business success through soft skills coaching. He coaches executives and entrepreneurs through CommonquestConsulting.Com. You can reach Hayward at 815-828-6500 or email him at info@commonquest.org. Visit him on the web at www.softskillsthatwow.com

Zaahir 'Dr. Z.' Hendricks is a holistic physician, author and professional speaker who helps individuals unleash the mental shackles holding them back and live up to their full potential. Known as the Mindset Coach, his programs and presentations offer step-by-step strategies to become the person you want to be. Zaahir is the author of the book Mindset Determines Outcome, an inspirational novel with powerful lessons to help you move forward in life. His online immersion program of the same name helps you rewire your brain to become a visionary, empowered leader. Download your free Mindset Report at www.mindsetspeaker.com.

Acknowledgements

It is difficult to create any literary work by yourself. I am thankful that there are a number of people in my life who helped me along in the process of writing this book. In particular I would like to thank:

My wife Julie for her undying love and support and for putting up with me during this project.

My children; Anne, Allison, Ed and Jessica for being an inspiration on overcoming adversity.

My sister Diane who is always there for me during good times and bad.

Jacob Singer (Twitter: @jacobcsinger) for editing this book and making it much better than it was at the start.

Anita Quinlan and Jim Feigh who helped proofread this book and provided feedback on its content.

The members of my Mastermind group: Zaahir Hendricks, Ken Kocher, Louis Kreppert, Paul Rak and Hayward Suggs. Thanks for your constant support and feedback and for keeping me on track.

Poli Garza, for designing an awesome cover.

www.ingramcontent.com/pod-product-compliance
Lightning Source LLC
Chambersburg PA
CBHW060018210326
41520CB00009B/935

Elmer G. Willyoung

Electrical and Scientific Instruments and Apparatus

November 20th, 1899

Elmer G. Willyoung

Electrical and Scientific Instruments and Apparatus
November 20th, 1899

ISBN/EAN: 9783337421366

Printed in Europe, USA, Canada, Australia, Japan

Cover: Foto ©berggeist007 / pixelio.de

More available books at **www.hansebooks.com**

ELECTRICAL

AND

SCIENTIFIC INSTRUMENTS

AND APPARATUS.

NOVEMBER 20th, 1899.

ELMER G. WILLYOUNG,
82-84 Fulton Street,
New York.

NOTICE.

In ordering from this catalogue give both catalogue number and designation of item.

Remit by New York Draft, Money Order or Express. Add 25 cents to face of all checks, except on New York or Philadelphia, to cover the collection charge made by the N. Y. Clearing House.

Customers unknown to us must give satisfactory New York or Philadelphia reference or send cash with order. Or, we will ship C. O. D. provided cash remittance be made of at least ⅓ the amount of order ; but *no orders less than $5.00 will be shipped C. O. D.*

Charges for collection and return of money on C. O. D. shipments must be borne by the customer.

Goods ordered sent by mail must be prepaid and the postage included in remittance.

Packing will be charged at cost. All goods will be packed with the utmost care, but we assume no responsibility for breakage or other damage after the goods leave our hands. We guarantee all goods strictly as represented.

PREFATORY.

TO my friends, customers and the scientific and technical public generally I desire to state that I have succeeded to the business established and built up by Messrs. WILLYOUNG & Co., Philadelphia, retaining all the "good will" of the same, and have removed the headquarters of this business to New York City at the address below. I have also made a close alliance with Messrs. FOOTE, PIERSON & Co., successors to the manufacturing department of the late firm of E. S. GREELEY Co., by which they pass over to me all the "good will," etc., of such measuring instrument business as they have been doing. By the terms of this arrangement all "Willyoung" apparatus as also all the "Greeley" measuring instruments will be made in the shops of FOOTE, PIERSON & Co., under my immediate direction and supervision and according to my design. To take care of this business the already extensive shops of this firm have been greatly added to in floor space during the past three months, while a large number of the most recent high class tools have also been installed. The shop and laboratory have been put in charge of those holding the same positions under WILLYOUNG & Co.

All exclusive sales agencies for "Willyoung" apparatus have been abolished, and such apparatus may now be obtained direct from me or from the trade generally. I believe this will be of real advantage to the public. There are often questions arising, either before or after a sale is made, which a salesman cannot answer—technical questions which he cannot be expected to answer. He must refer them to the inventor, designer or manufacturer. This means delay, possible errors due to faulty transmission of the information through a second party, and expense, on account of this extra and superfluous correspondence, which, in the long run, the customer must certainly pay for. Should the purchaser write direct to the manufacturer, but purchase of the sales agent, there is certain to result confusion and annoyance all around.

Having been largely active in the beginning and development of fine instrument manufacturing in America, and having been associated with it for a number of years past, I feel that myself and my apparatus is now so well known as to require here no special sounding of trumpets.

All the instruments and apparatus in this catalogue have been very thoroughly revised during the Summer past, and every possible improvement as regards construction and convenience in manipulation has been effected. The entire line of instruments, therefore, is thoroughly up to date.

This catalogue has been prepared with great care and it is believed that the errors, if any, are extremely few in number. So far as possible the various instruments are brought under a logical classification. Each class is prefaced by succinct information as to the place of this class in the general scheme of instrumental work, and the general method of use required by the features which differentiate the individual types under a general group. It is believed that this information will be valued and will be found extremely useful in facilitating intelligent selection on the part of many customers.

The manufacture of two grades of apparatus, viz., Grade A and Grade B, has met with such unqualified approval on the part of the public that it is continued.

Grade A applies to apparatus finished throughout in the best possible manner. Apparatus of Grade B is guaranteed equal to Grade A in all essential respects (material, general workmanship and accuracy of adjustment), but does not present the same highly polished and beautiful exterior. As most instruments soon show the effect of use, Grade B is very popular and is purchased in preference to Grade A in the large majority of cases.

My facilities for the manufacture of all kinds of special apparatus, whether from customers or my own design, cannot be surpassed.

A force of men is continually engaged in making repairs. I can do such work reasonably and promptly. Many instruments now useless could be given an effective lease of life with a little alteration.

My system of data relating to instruments and measurements has been carefully and accurately kept for many years back. There are few instruments or measurements ever suggested which I cannot locate. This information is at the service of my customers.

I make my instruments as well as I know how; study them carefully always. But I do not know it all and I sometimes make mistakes. I welcome suggestions or criticisms and know that such will enable me to turn out a better product.

A picture always shows more than a description, and I would like to have **every** instrument illustrated; but this is commercially impossible. I do have, however, photographs of nearly everything made by me, and I shall be glad to send one to any interested party to whom the catalogue description is inadequate.

ELMER G. WILLYOUNG.

NEW YORK, November 20th, 1899.

KEY TO REFERENCES USED.

C. & P.	Carhart & Patterson's "Electrical Measurements."
Ayrton.	Ayrton's "Practical Electricity," 3d Ed.
Palaz.	"Treatise on Industrial Photometry," by Palaz ; translated from the French by Patterson.
S. & G.	Stewart & Gee's "Elementary Practical Physics," Vol. II.
Henderson.	Henderson's "Practical Electricity and Magnetism."
Gray.	"Absolute Measurements in Electricity and Magnetism," two volumes, by A. Gray.
Phil. Mag.	"London and Edinburgh Philosophical Magazine and Journal of Science."
Kempe.	Kempe's "Hand-book of Electrical Testing." Fifth Edition

ELECTRICAL CONDENSERS.

Electrical Condenser—The combination consisting of a conducting surface brought near to a second similar surface and separated therefrom by an insulating medium. The conducting surface may take the form of flat plates, concentric spheres or cylinders, or any one of a variety of other forms.

Capacity.—May be defined as the quantity of electricity required to raise the potential of a condenser from zero to unity.

Let C=Capacity of a condenser

V=P. D. between the condenser plates.

Q=Quantity of electricity with which the condenser is charged.

Then, by definition :

$$C= \frac{Q}{V} \dots\dots\dots\dots\dots\dots\dots\dots\dots\dots\dots\dots\dots\dots\dots\dots\dots\dots\dots(1)$$

The Unit of Capacity—Let Q=One Coulomb=10^{-1} C.G. S. units.

V=One Volt $\quad=10^8$ " "

Then $C=\frac{10^{-1}}{10^8}=10^{-9}$ C. G. S. Units=One FARAD or F.

The Micro-Farad—The Farad being vastly larger than the capacities ordinarily met with the MICRO-FARAD, or $\frac{\text{FARAD}}{1,000,000}$ has been chosen as the practical working unit of capacity.

Hence 1 M. F.=10^{-15} C. G. S Units.

Specific Inductive Capacity — In a general way the capacity of a condenser increases directly with the area of conducting surface and inversely as the distance which separates the two surfaces. It also varies with the particular insulating medium (dielectric), being a minimum for air. In a given condenser, therefore, the ratio of capacity with a given dielectric to the capacity with air is known as the SPECIFIC INDUCTIVE CAPACITY =k= of the dielectric.

Working Forms of Condensers — In practice two general classes of condensers are used. Those of fixed and known capacity for use as standards in quantitative work and those of large but not necessarily known capacity for use in qualitative experiments. We may further sub-divide, as below :

A—Standard Air Condensers ; here the dielectric is air. The conductors are generally simple geometric forms as e. g., two concentric cylinders whose dimensions, etc., may be exactly determined and the capacity thus be arrived at. Such condensers are, hence, often known as *Absolute Condensers*. Their capacity is relatively small owing to the low S. I. C. of air.

B—Standard Mica Condensers. Here the dielectric is mica ; generally the condenser is built up of alternate layers of mica and tin foil, every other sheet of foil being joined together to make one coating while the remaining sheets constitute the other coating. Condensers of this class are used for 99% of the measuring work of the world.

C—Paper Condensers. These are similar to " B." save that paper saturated with some insulating mixture is used as a dielectric. Both as regards insulation and "absorption" these condensers are inferior to the mica condensers of " B."

D—High Potential Condensers ; for use in work with high frequency, high potential discharges from transformer or static machine. The dielectric is thick glass and the conductors of copper foil. The whole is then immersed in oil or covered with insulating wax. On account of the extreme thickness of insulation required the capacity is necessarily small.

Condensers in Multiple or Series—The capacity of a number of condensers joined in *multiple* is expressed by

$$C = C_1 + C_2 + C_3 + \text{etc} \dots\dots\dots\dots\dots\dots\dots\dots\dots\dots\dots\dots (2)$$

If the condensers are placed in *series*, their capacity becomes

$$C = \cfrac{1}{\dfrac{1}{C_1} + \dfrac{1}{C_2} + \dfrac{1}{C_3} + \text{etc.}} \dots\dots\dots\dots\dots\dots\dots\dots\dots\dots\dots (3)$$

It will be noted that (2) is the formula for resistances in *series*, and (3) for resistances in *multiple*.

Multiple Combinations for Varying Capacities Through Wide Ranges—If there be sets of four condensers, each having the proper values for each decimal place, and the connections be so arranged that any multiple combination of the condensers may be effected, then capacities varying by 1 part in 10, 100. 1,000, etc., according to the number of sets of four condensers used, may be obtained,

In a 3-bank condenser the individual capacities may be

				Sum.
1st bank,	.001,	.002.	.002,	.005 = .01
2d bank,	.01,	.02,	.02,	.05 = .10
3d bank,	.1,	.2,	.2,	.5 =1.00
Total,				1.11

The above combinations will give capacities varying by .001th from .001 to 1.11. If all are placed in series, they have a capacity .0004095, which is practically $\frac{1}{2500}$.

Uses for the Mica Condenser — A high-class Standard Mica Condenser is especially adapted for

(1) The calibration of a ballistic galvanometer

(2) The measurement of exceedingly high resistances by "leakage" methods ; these are largely used in insulation tests of submarine and high pressure transmission cables.

(3) The measurement of E. M. F's, particularly those of batteries subject to quick polarization.